Photos for Creative Purposes
Animals

Rosie Hartmann

Copyright © 2019 Rosie M. Hartmann

All rights reserved.
Printed in the United States of America

First Printing, 2019

ISBN: 978-1-948326-10-0

Hello, Creatives!

Over the last 15 years, photography has been a mainstay in my world. During that time my creative endeavors have led me to many types of art mediums. Each time I learn a new medium I come to understand the greater role photography has for other creatives who are not photographers.

Collage artists, in some cases, need copyright-free photography for use in their work. At the same time, painters might like to work off reference photos and there are those who practice Soul Collage as a method of self-discovery. I include visual journal creators, crafters, those who upcycle furniture and many others who require this type of photography. Indeed, I have tried many of these things myself. I would have been lost without having my archives of photography to draw from.

Add this to my knowledge that all creative things just want to be out in the world doing their thing. Books want their pages turned, photos want to be seen/used and visual art wants to be experienced. Within this book are images that want to be cut out, used and/or torn up if needed. Within this book are images that can be freely used. With your endeavors, these images will fulfill their purpose. Hopefully, they can help you fulfill yours as well.

Once you are done, take what you have created from these images and share it with the world if you so desire. Approach all these possibilities with JOY. As Robert Henri said, "All real works of art look as though there were done in Joy".

Happy & Joyful Creating to you!
Rosie
www.StudioRosie.com
Facebook: @StudioRosie

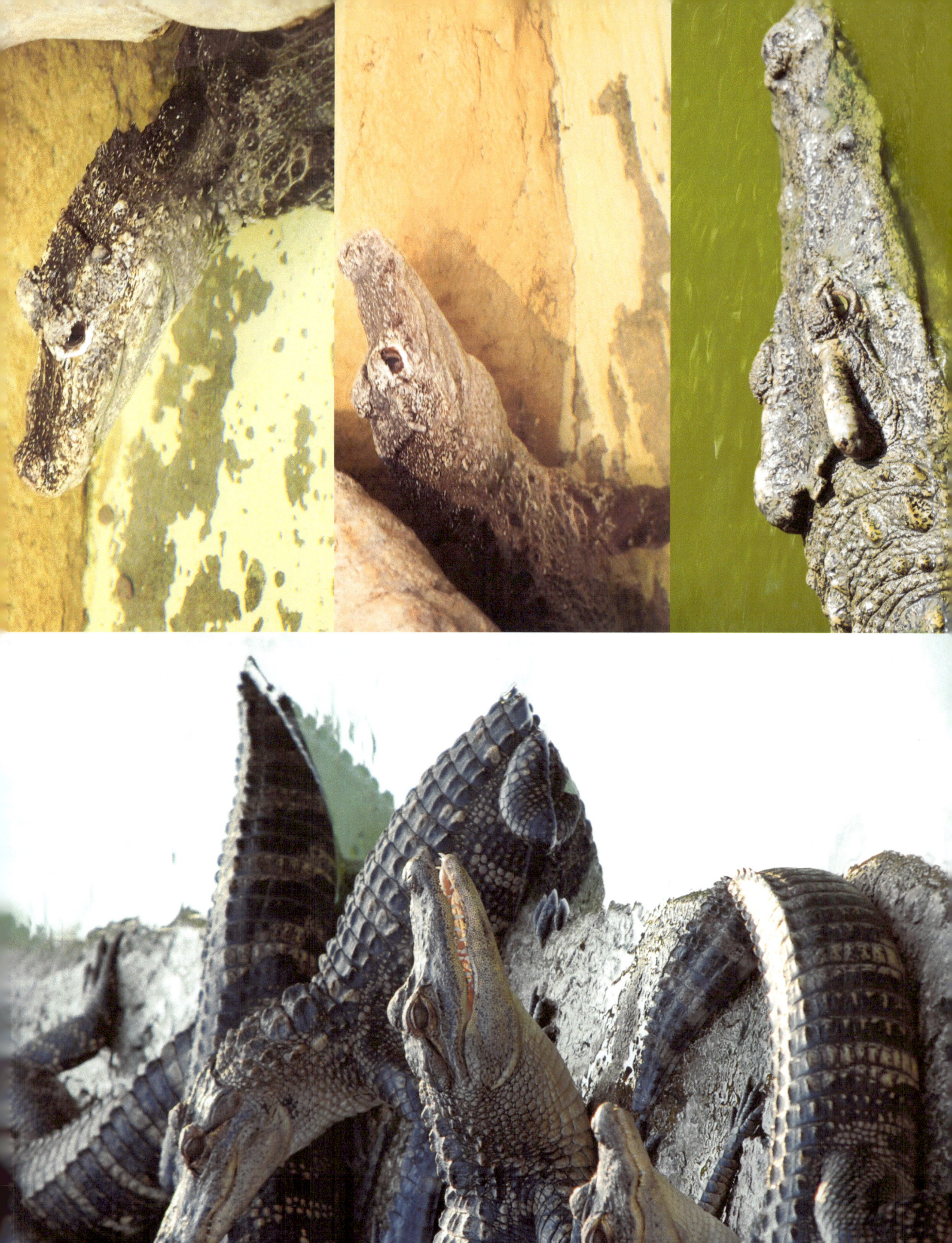

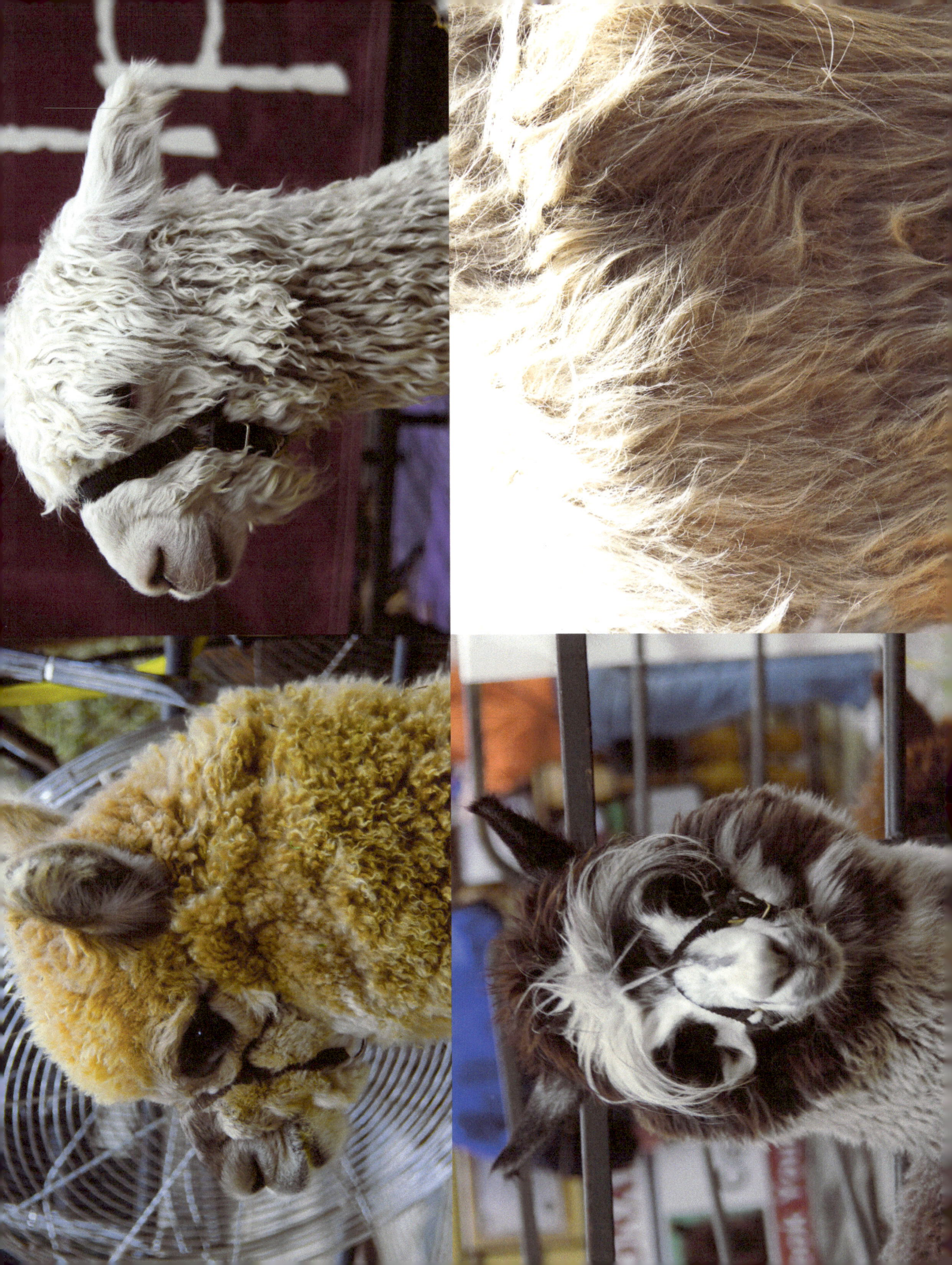

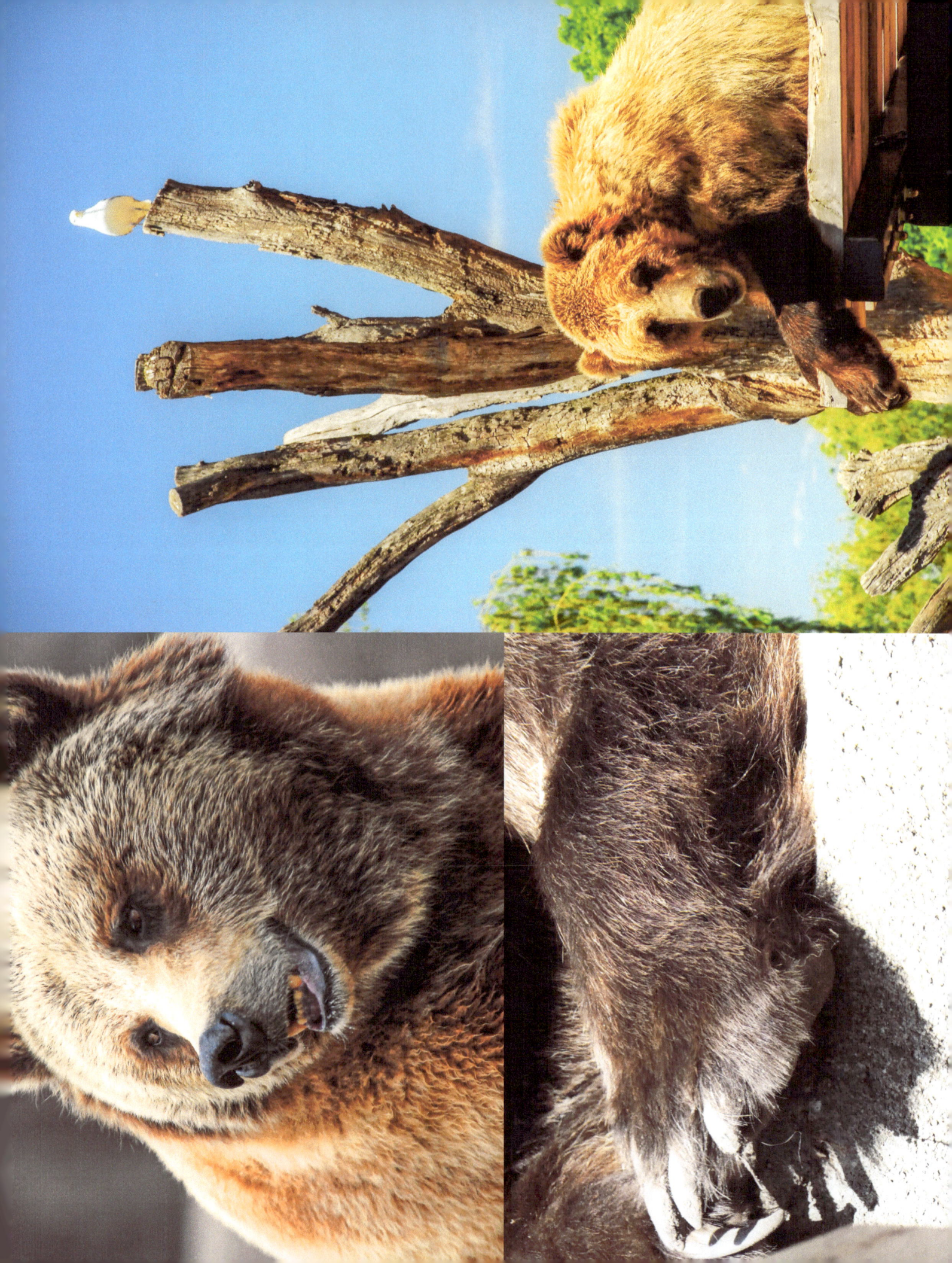

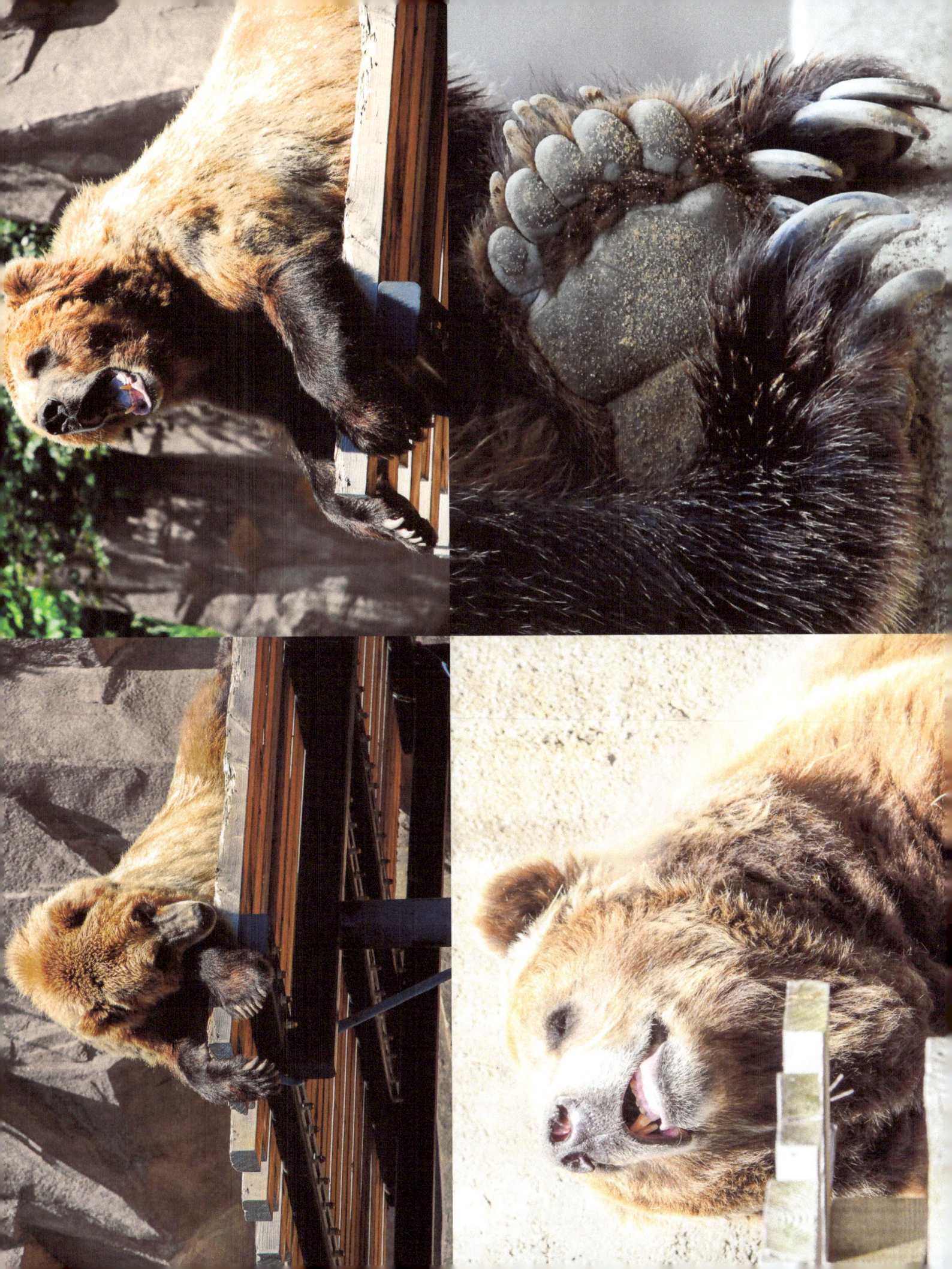

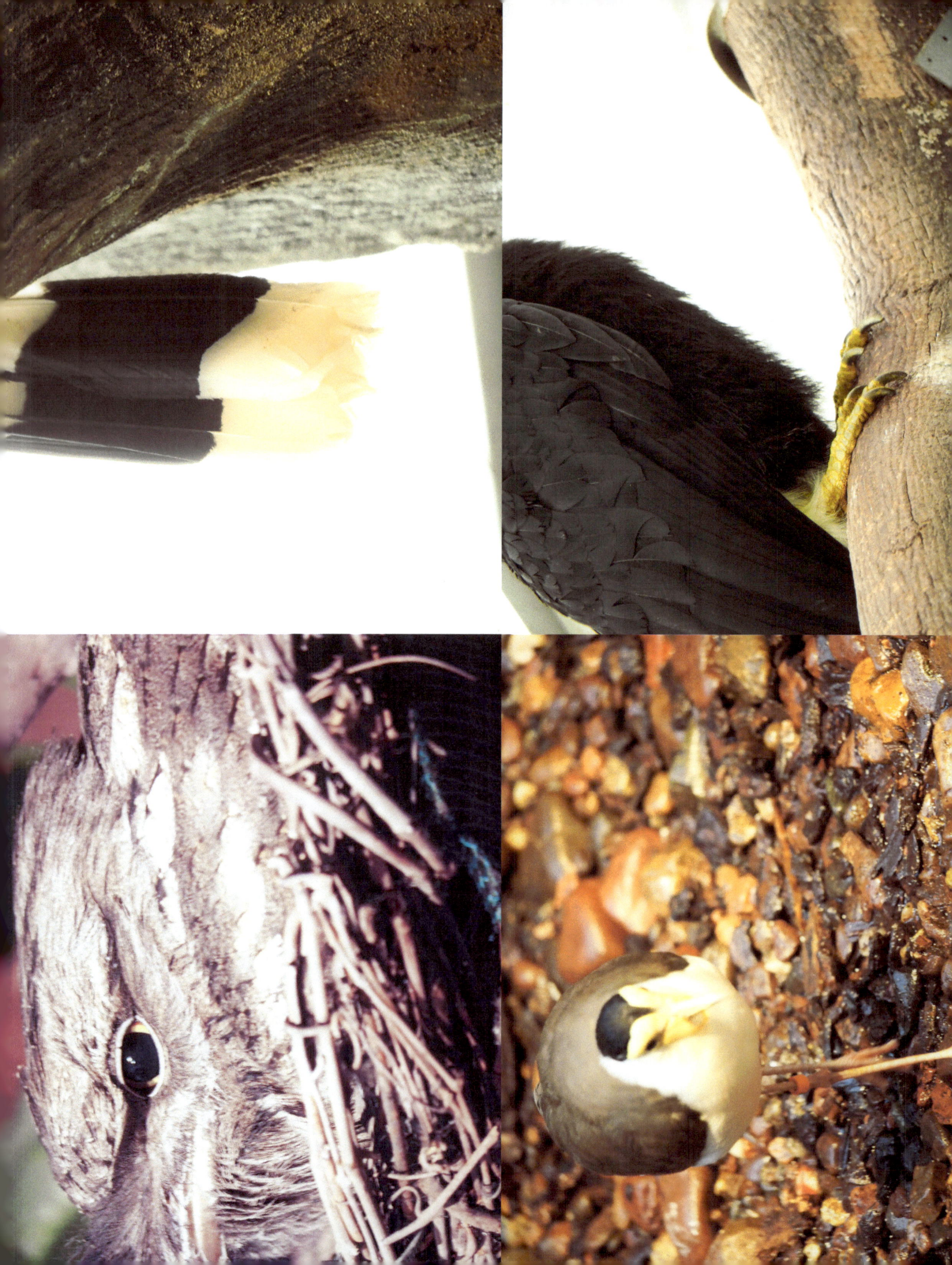

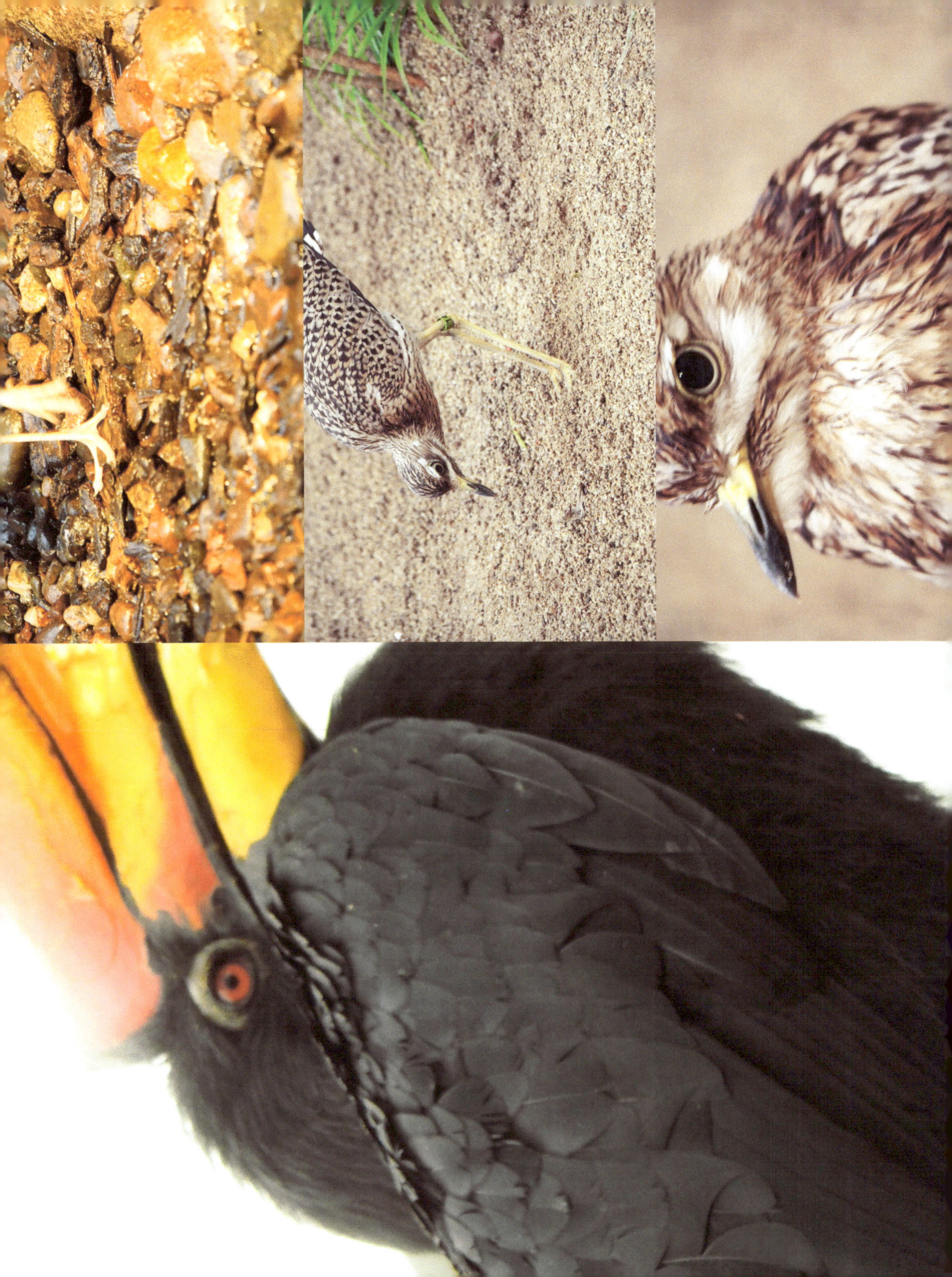

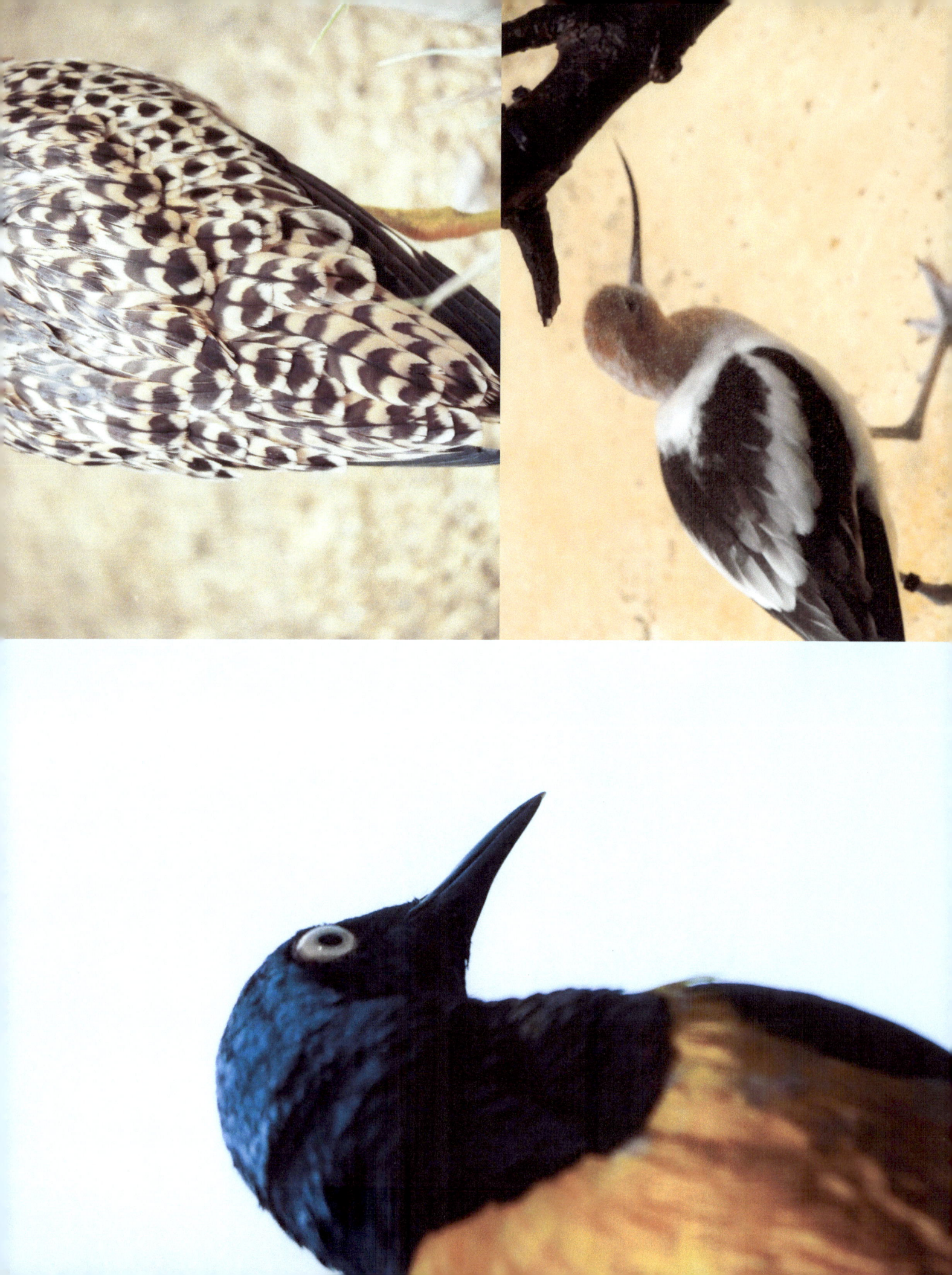

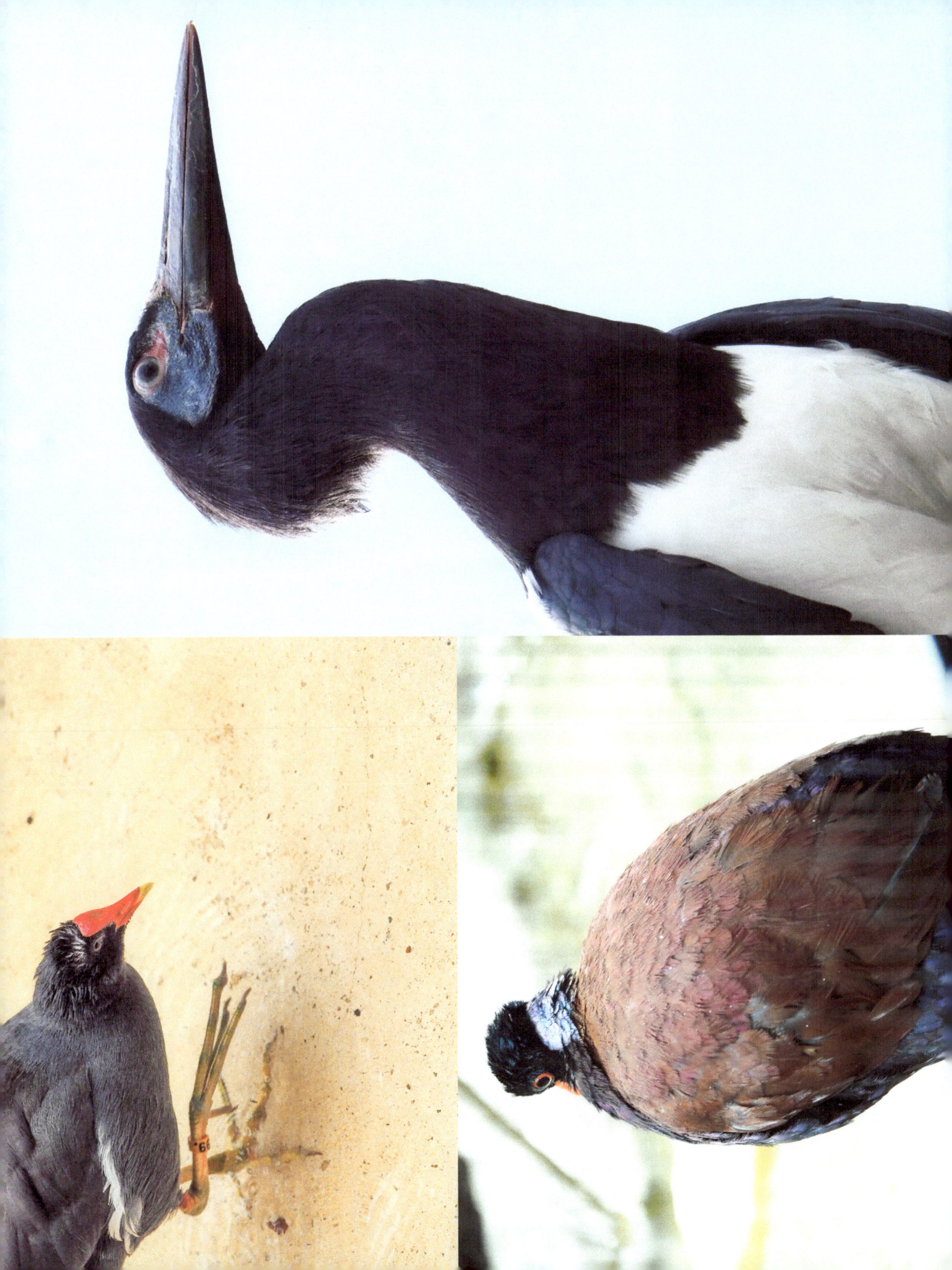

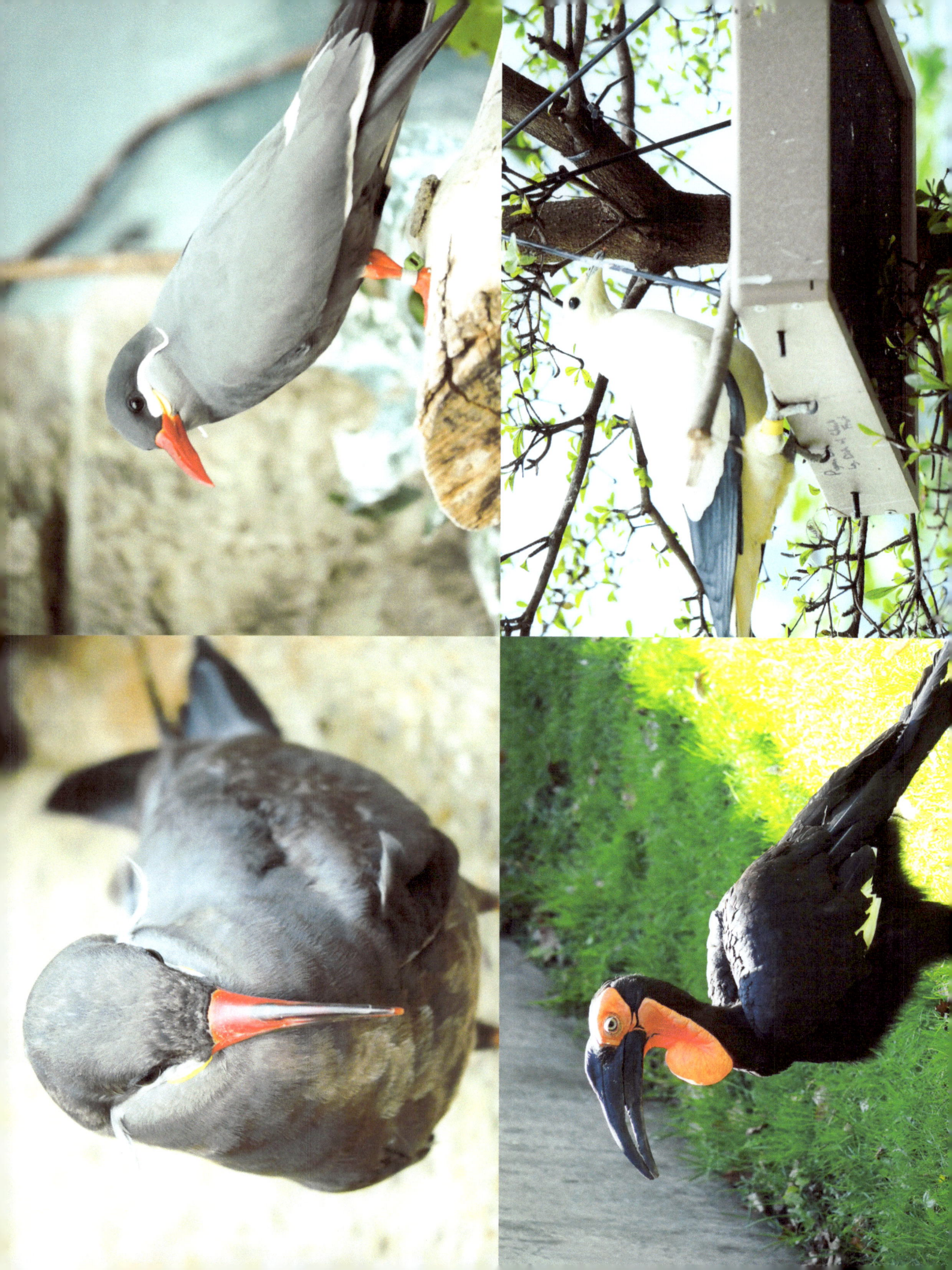

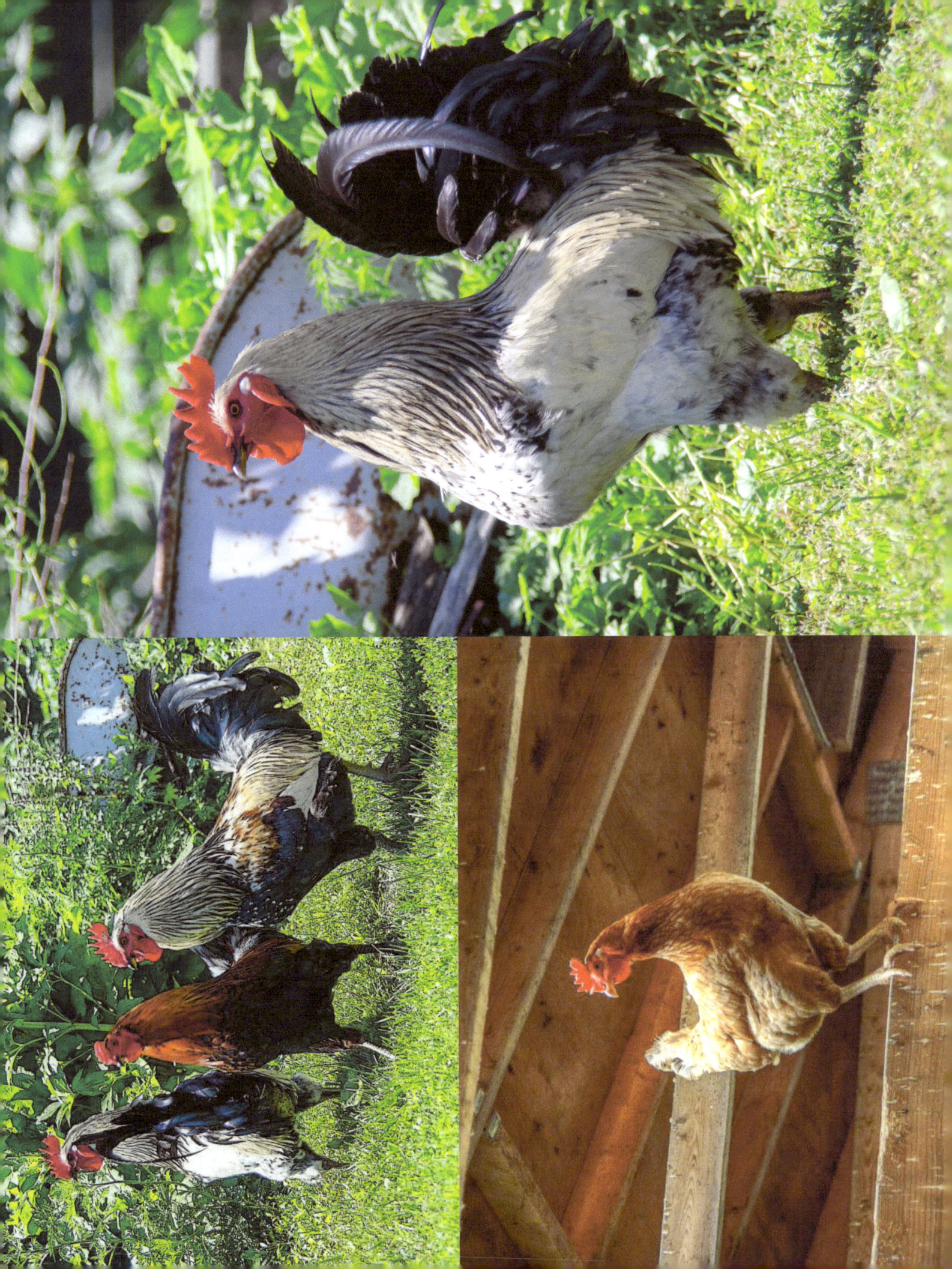

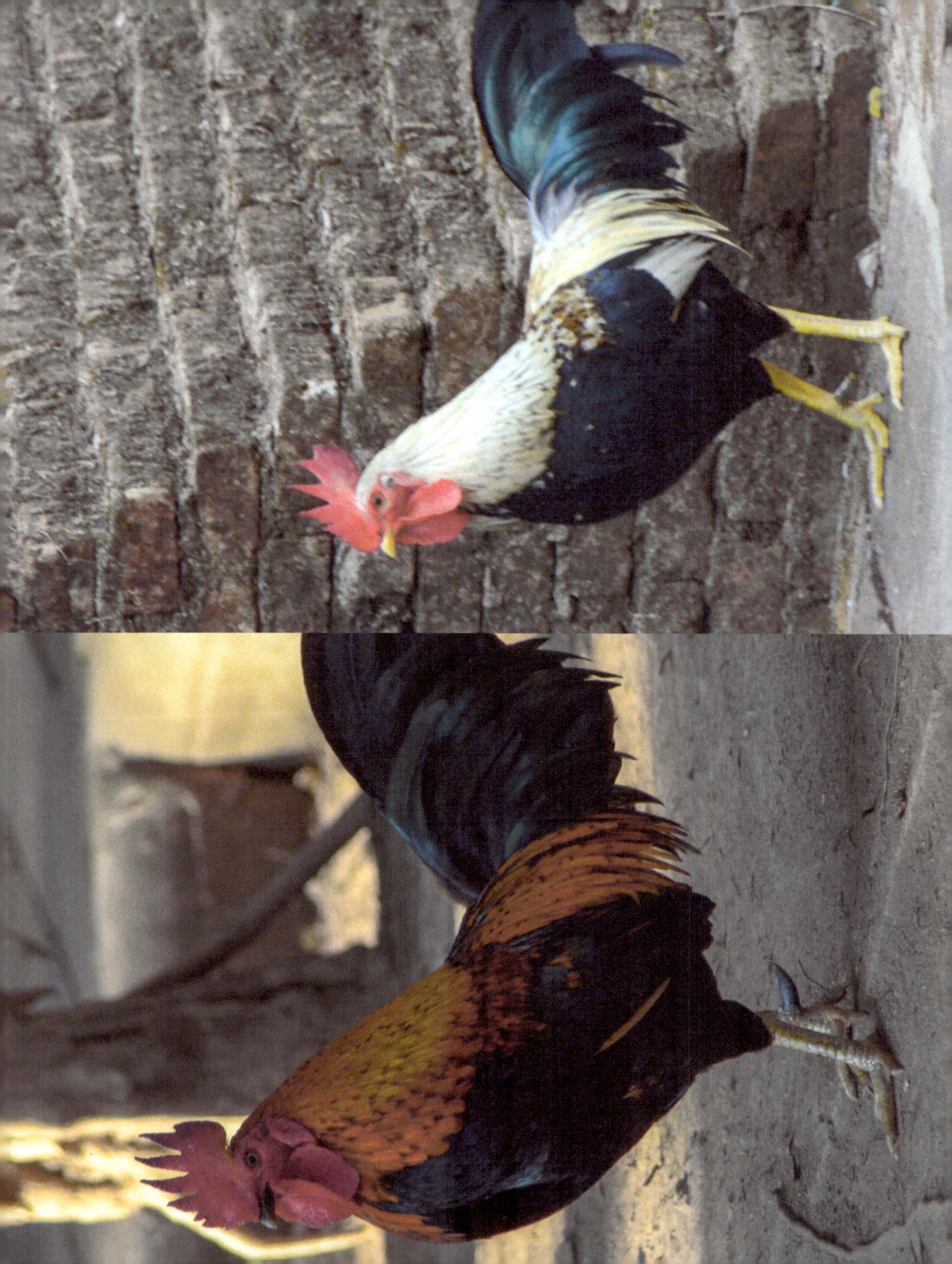

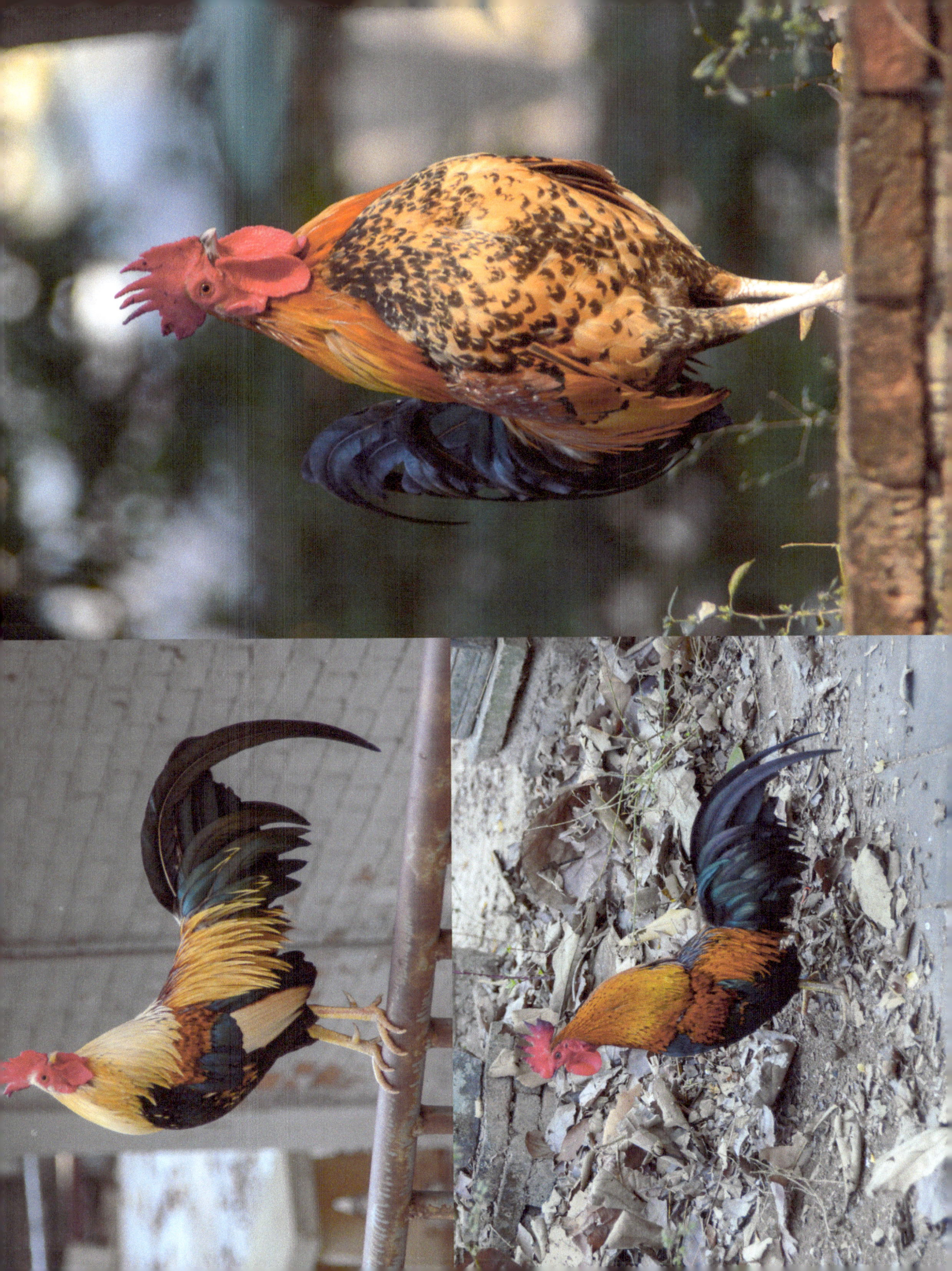

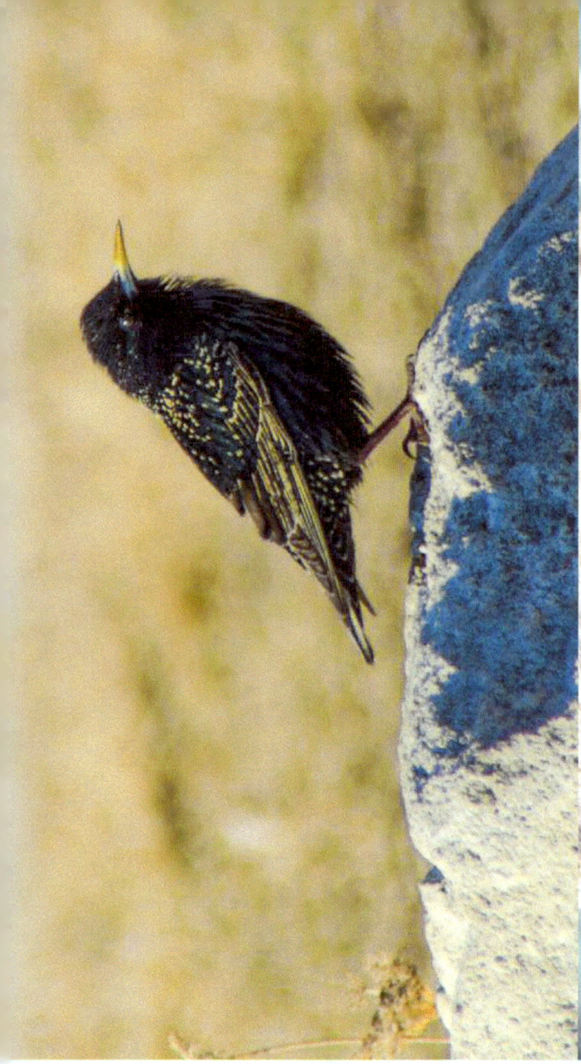

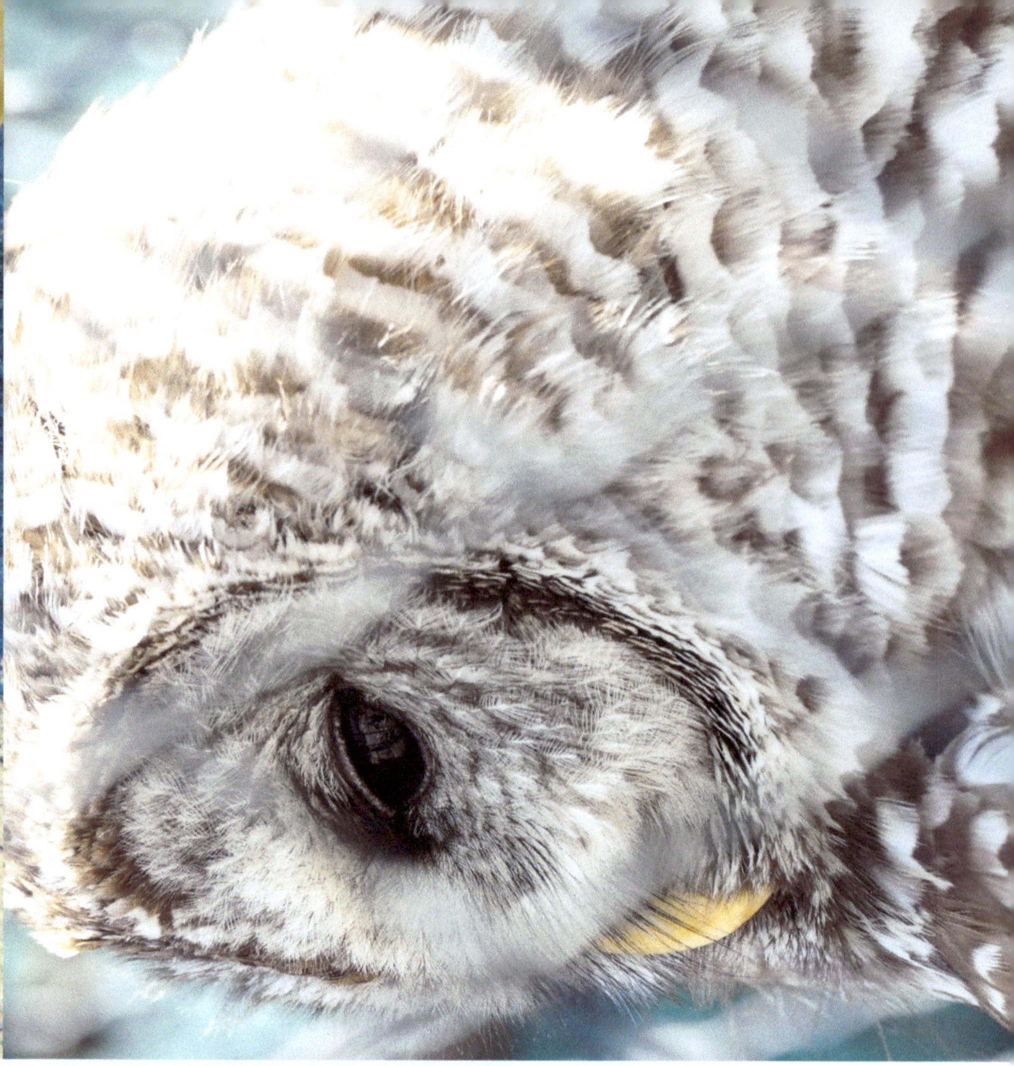

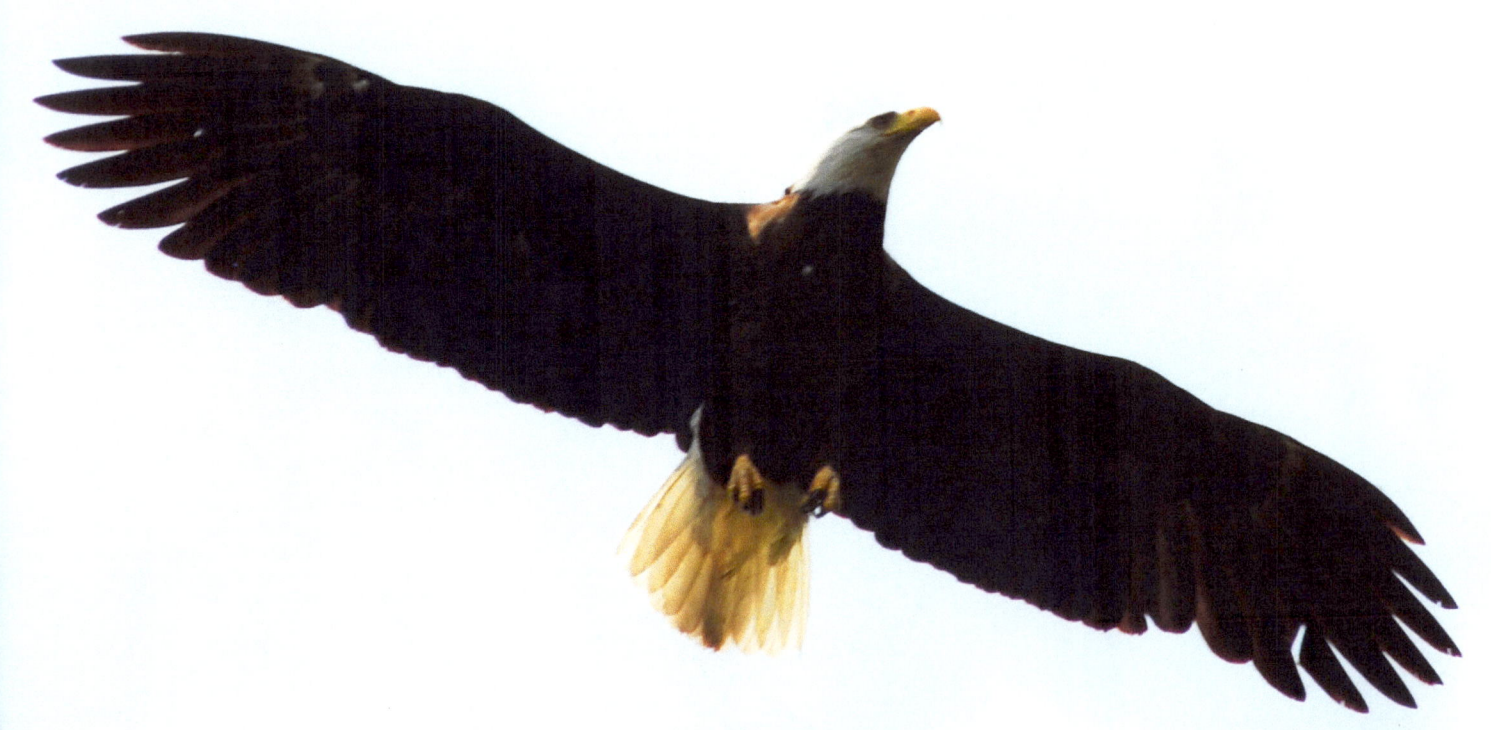

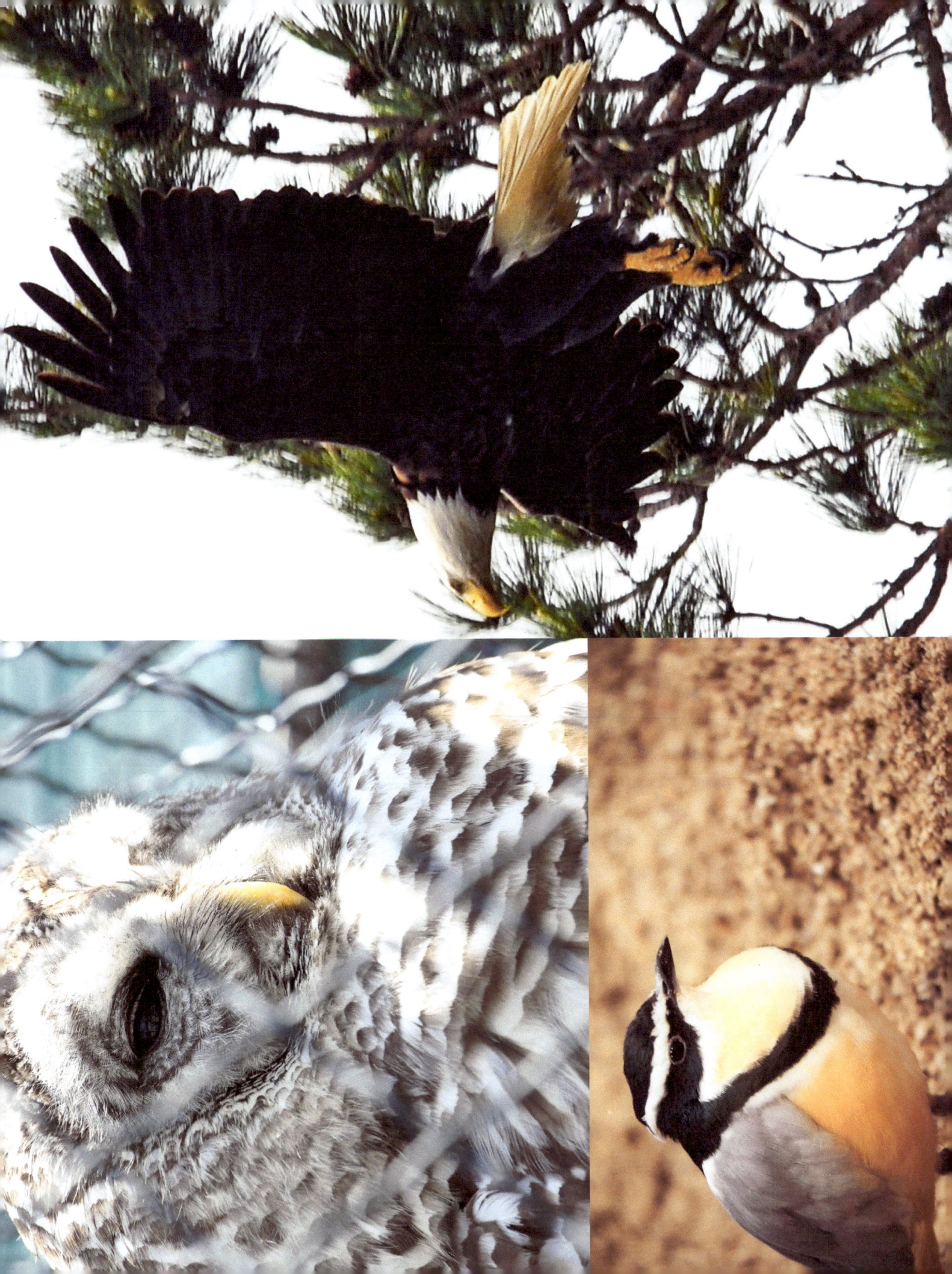

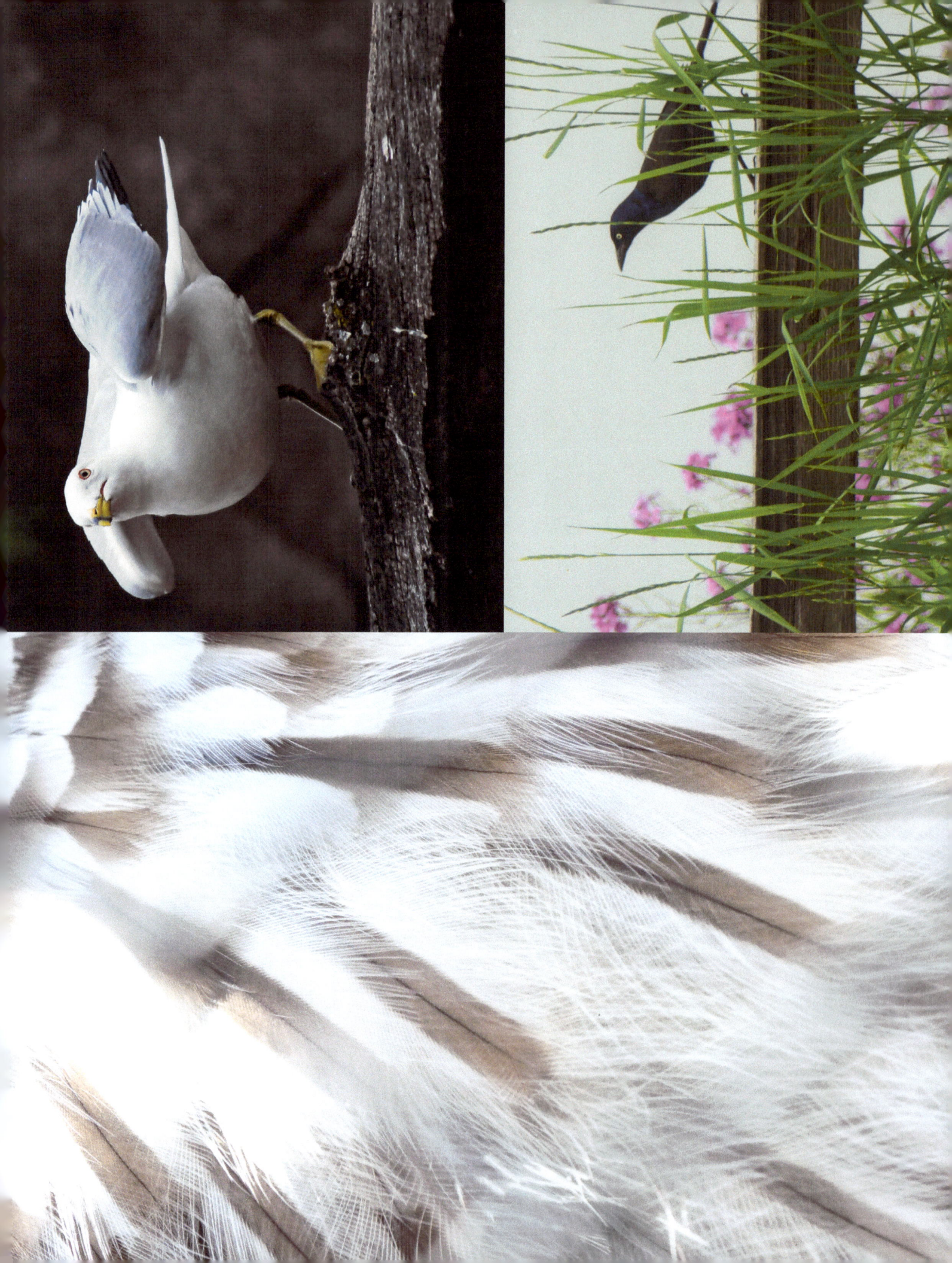

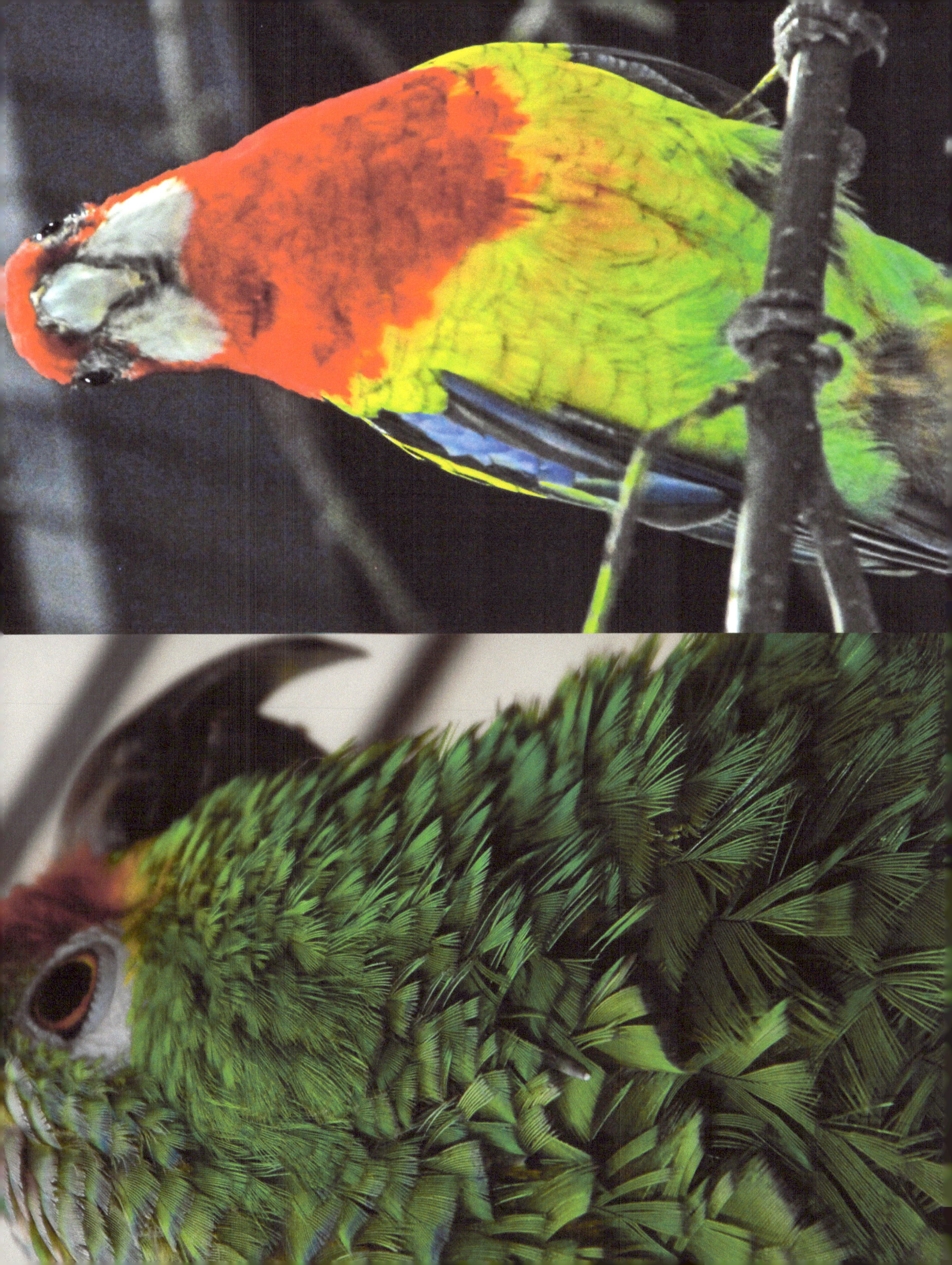

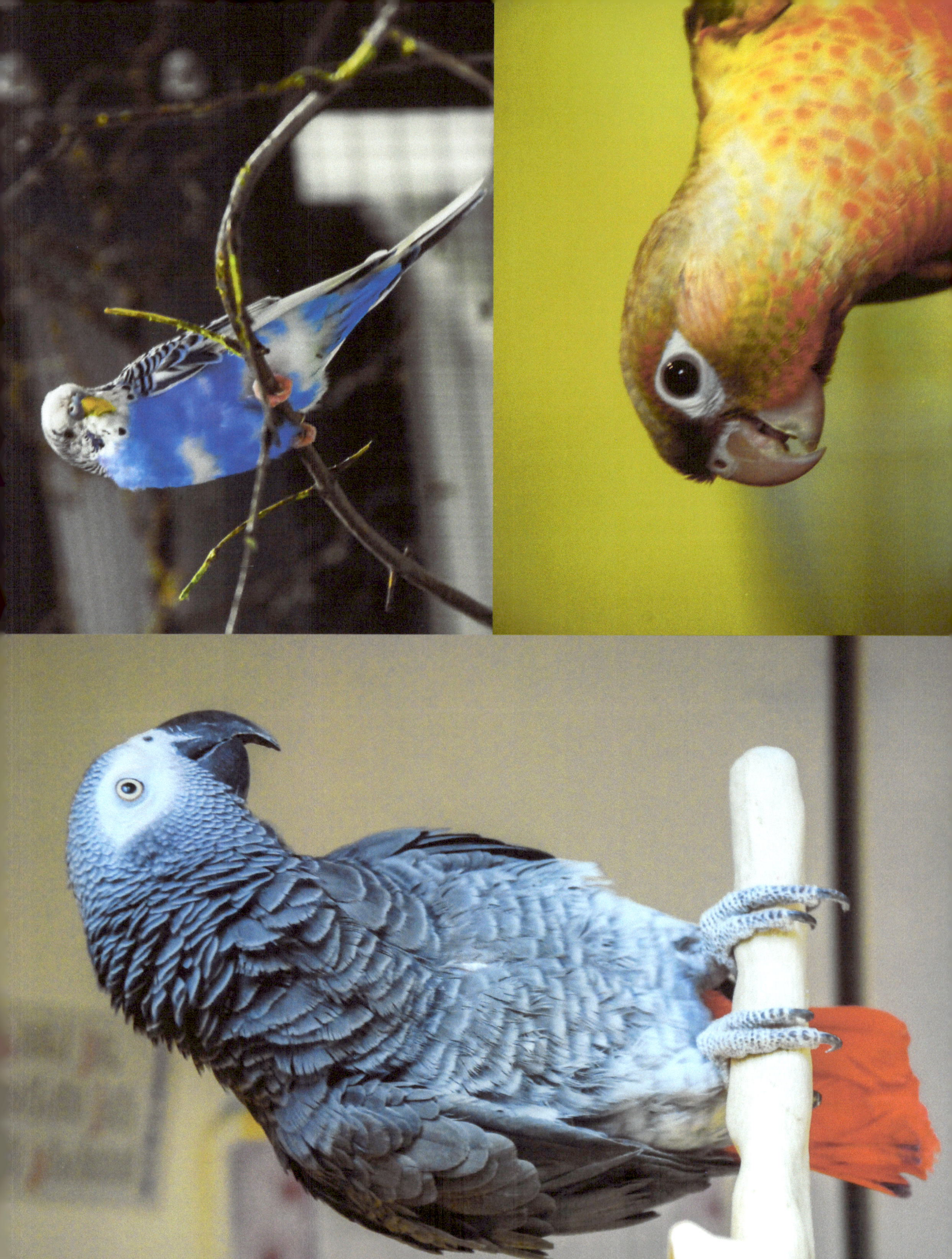

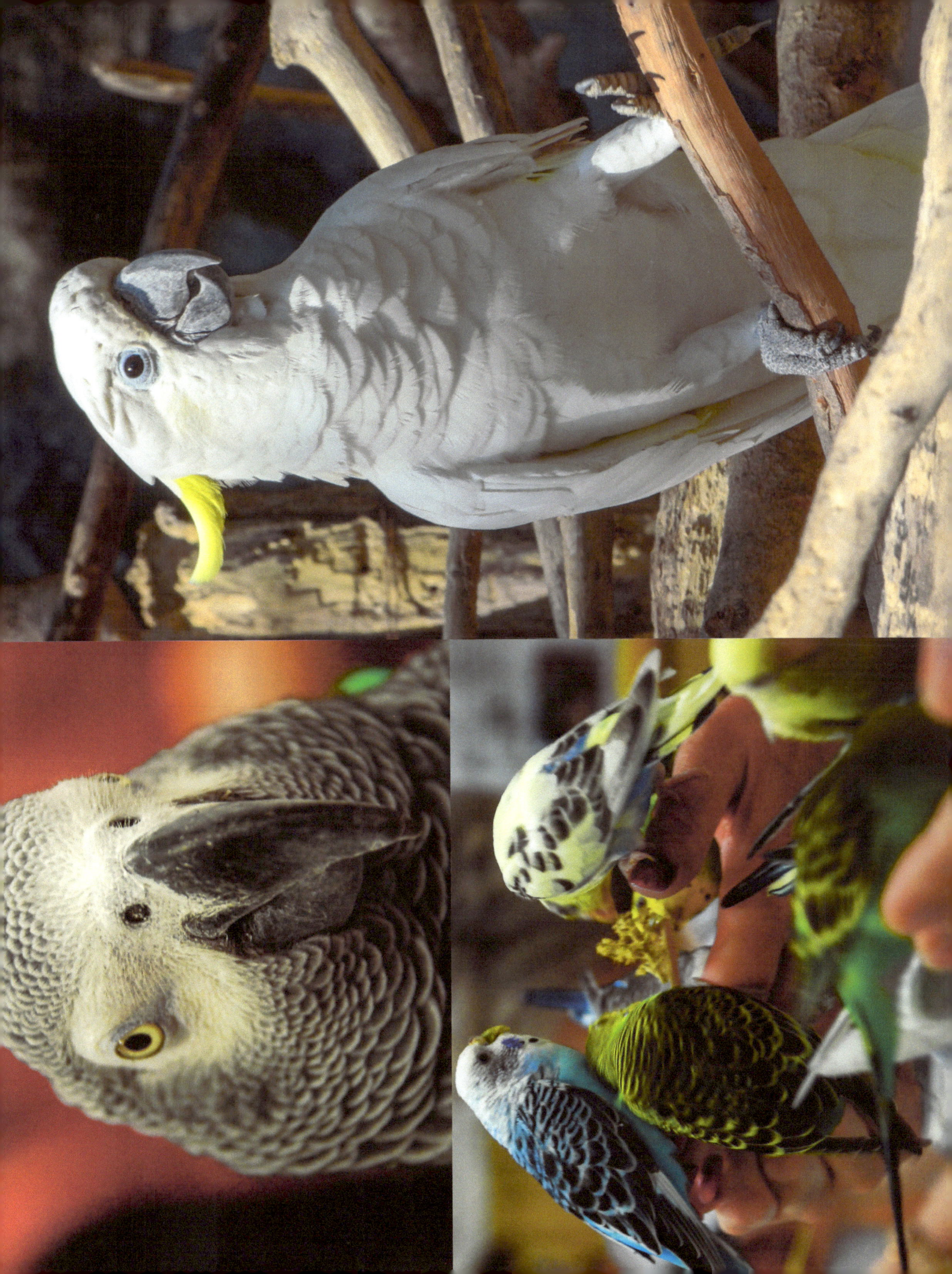

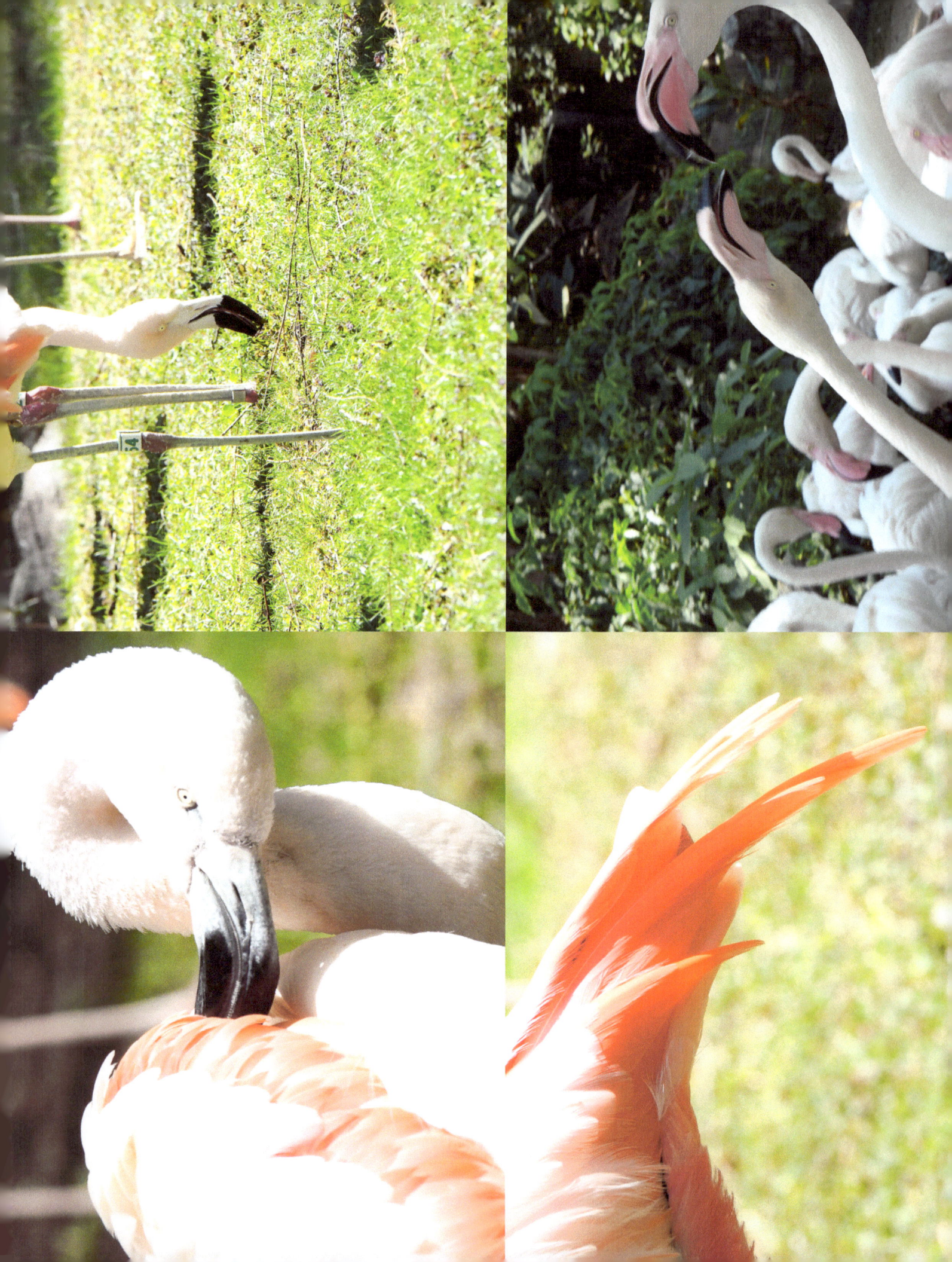

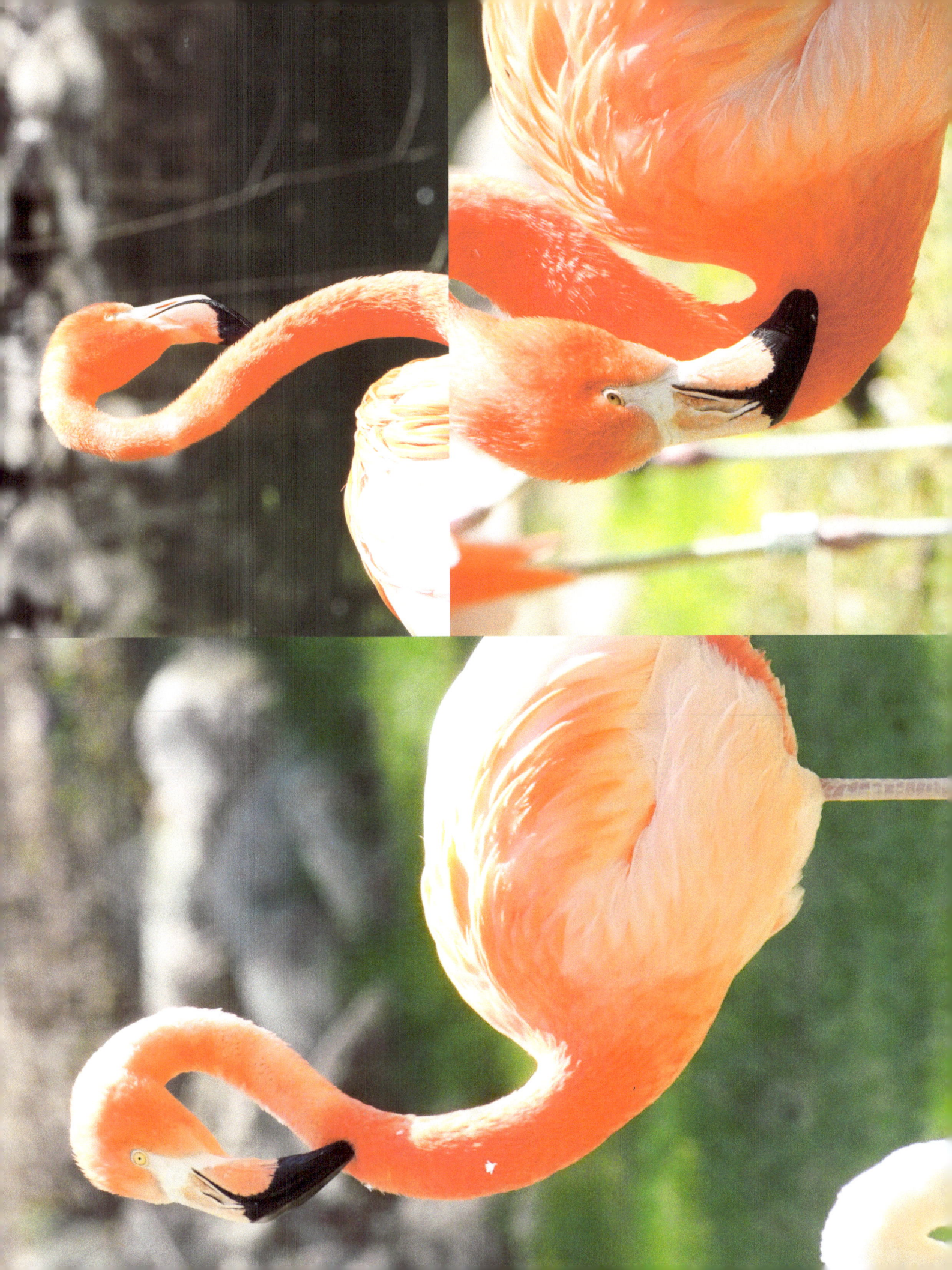

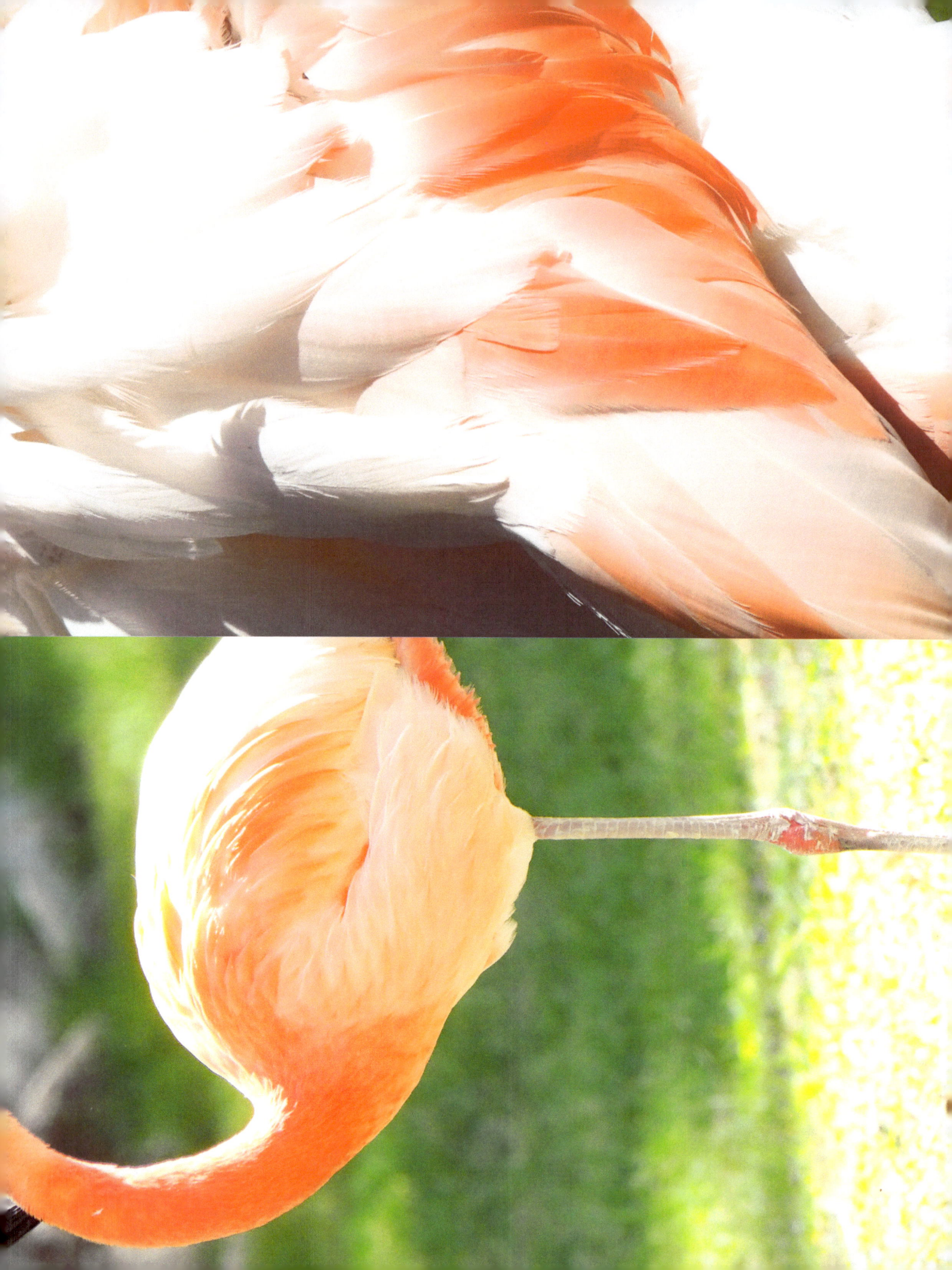

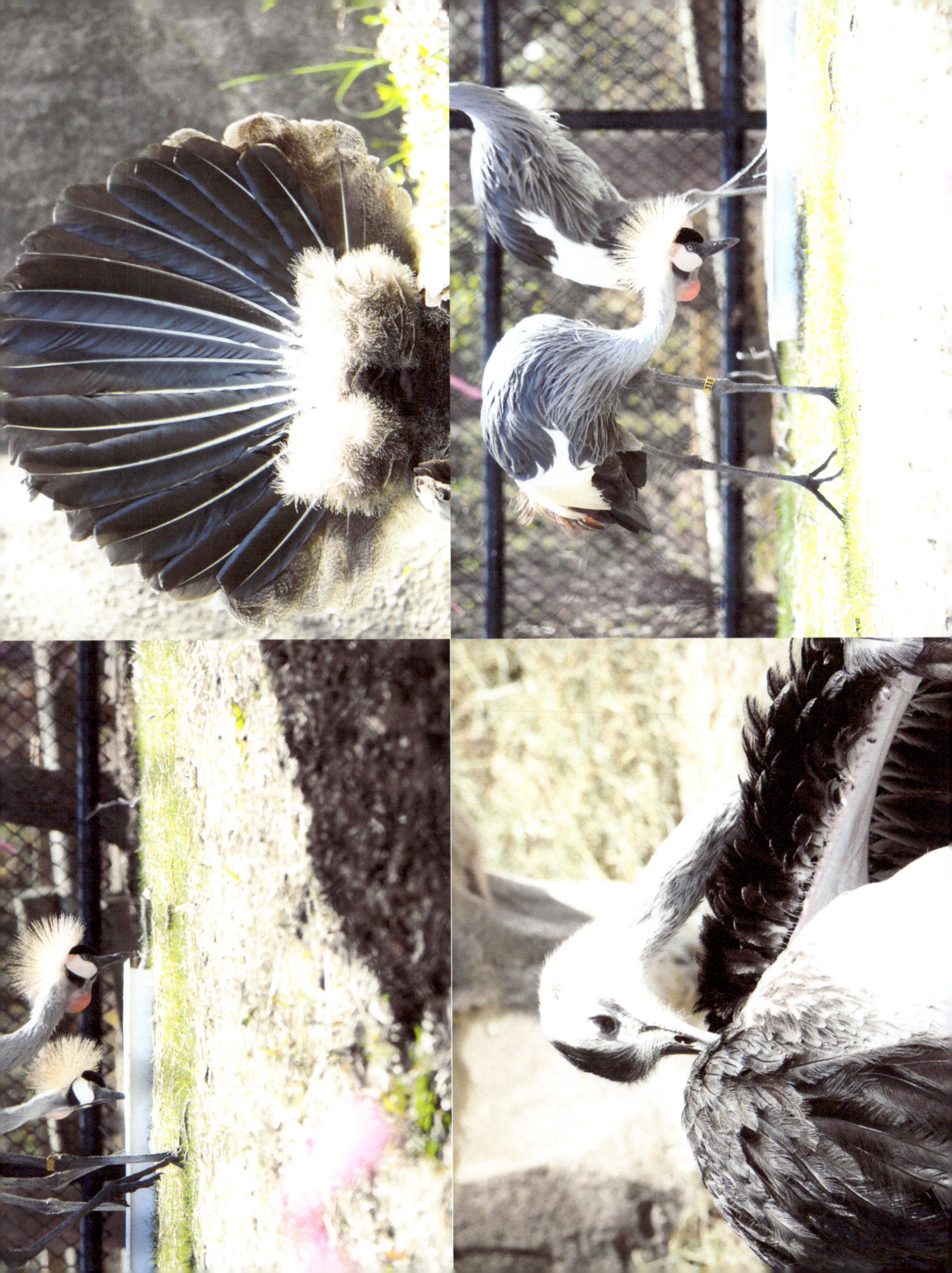

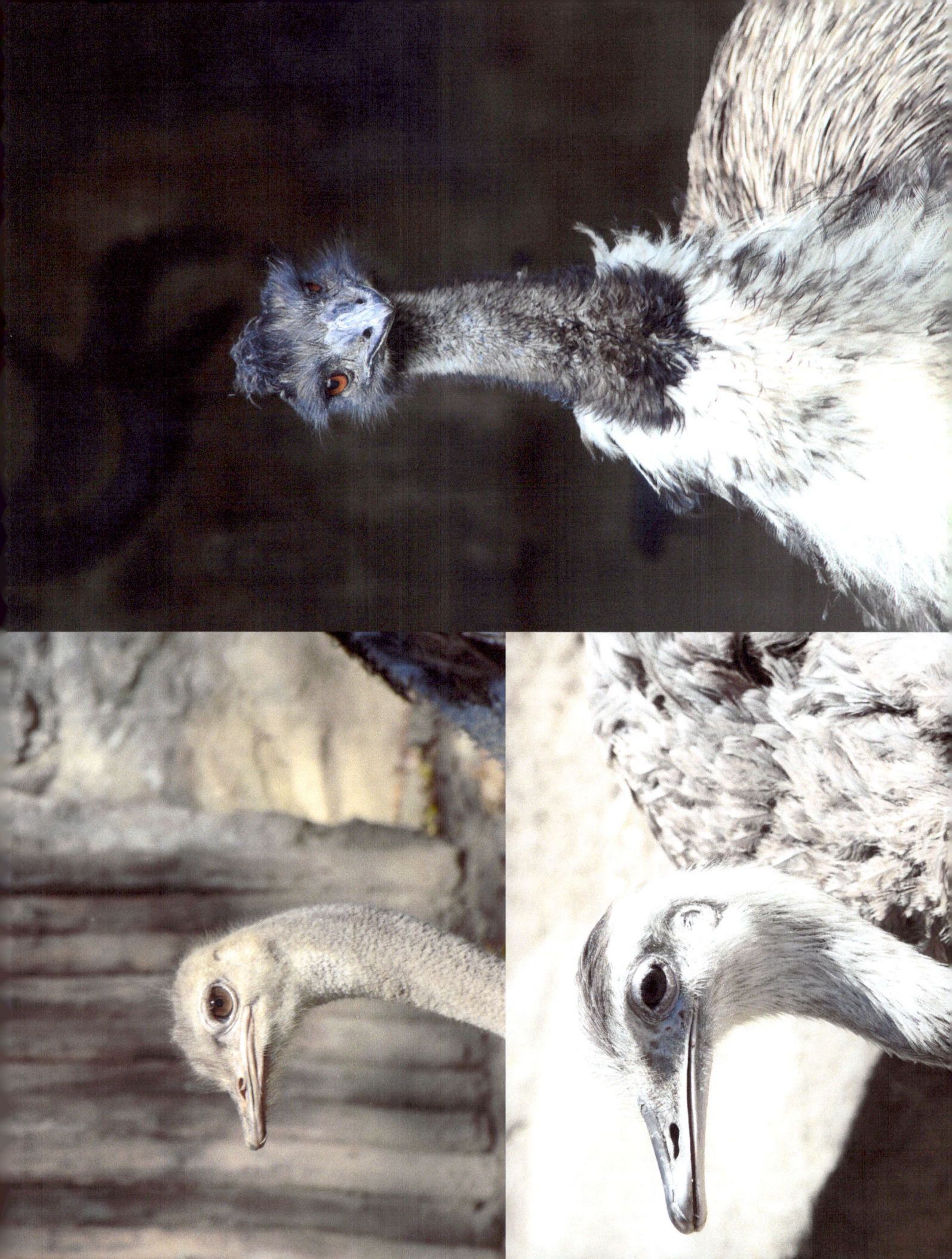

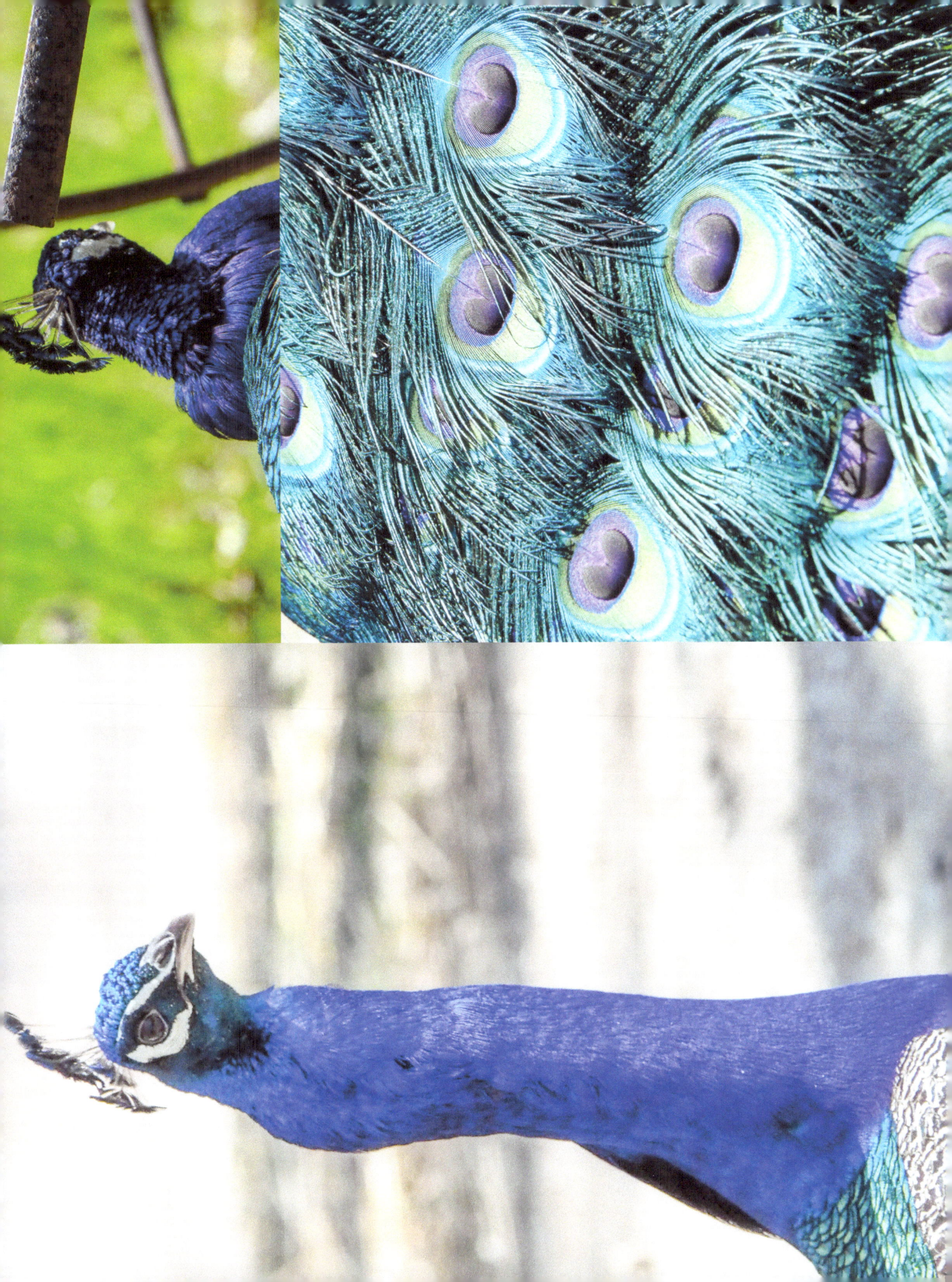

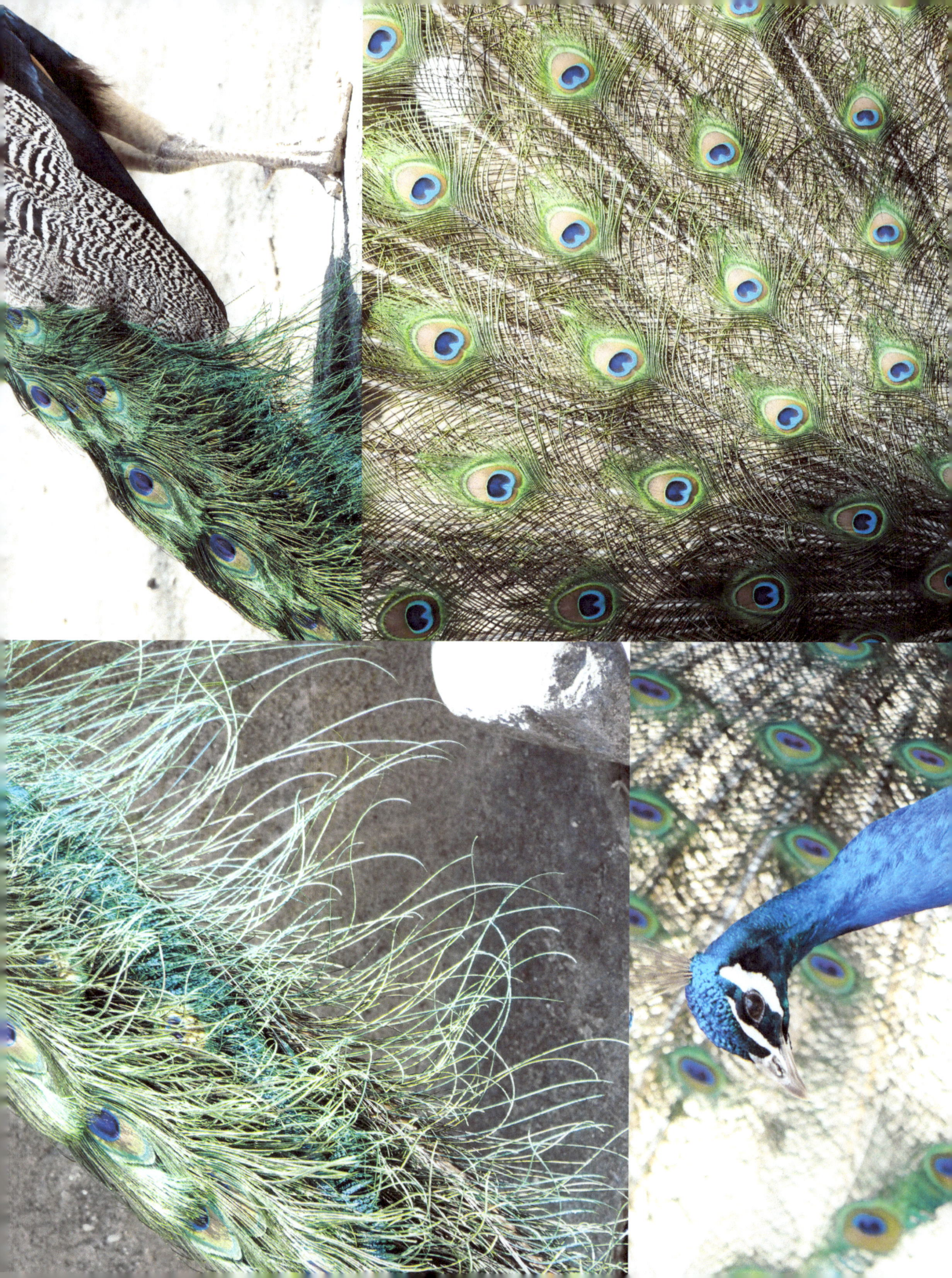

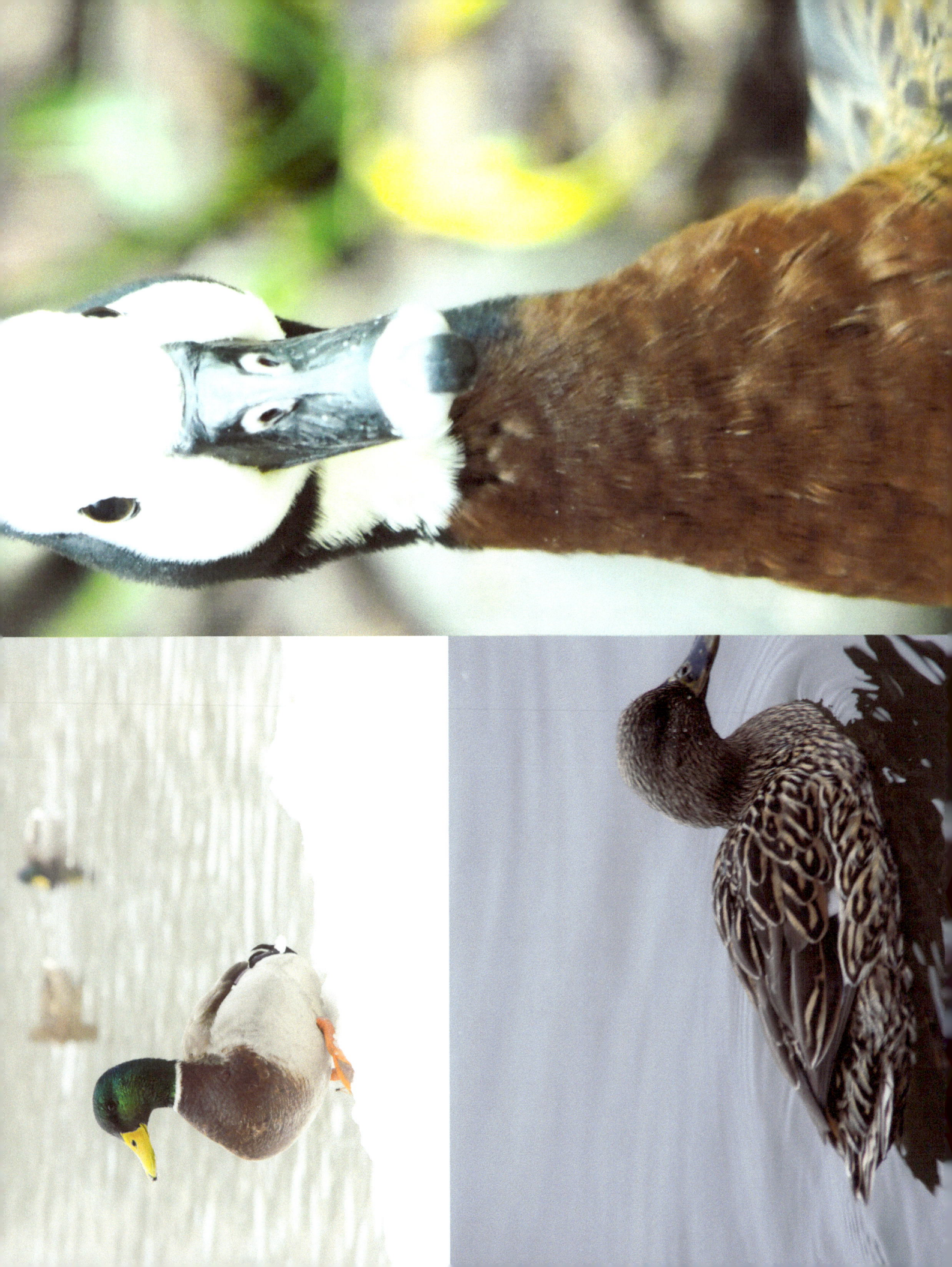

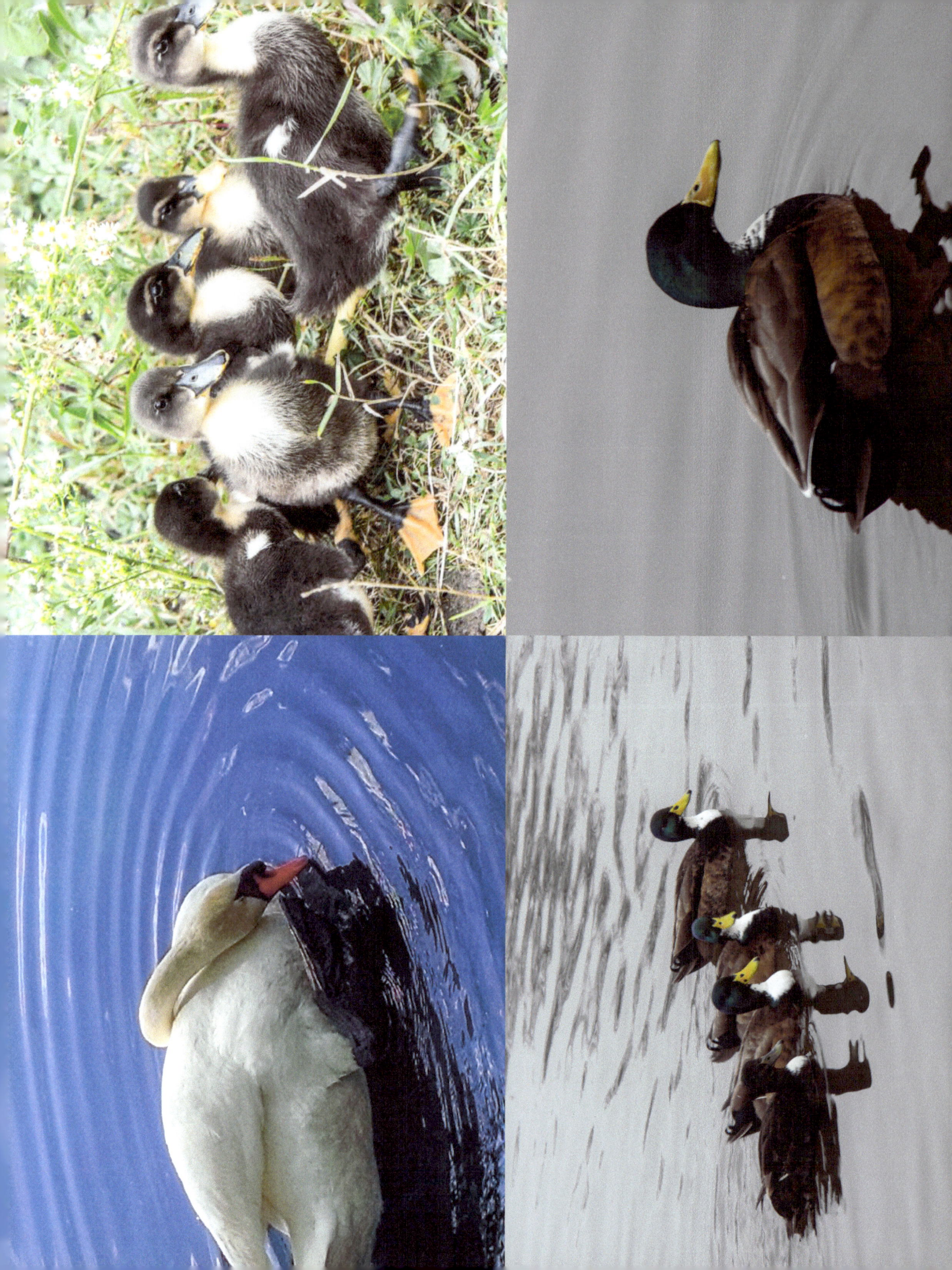

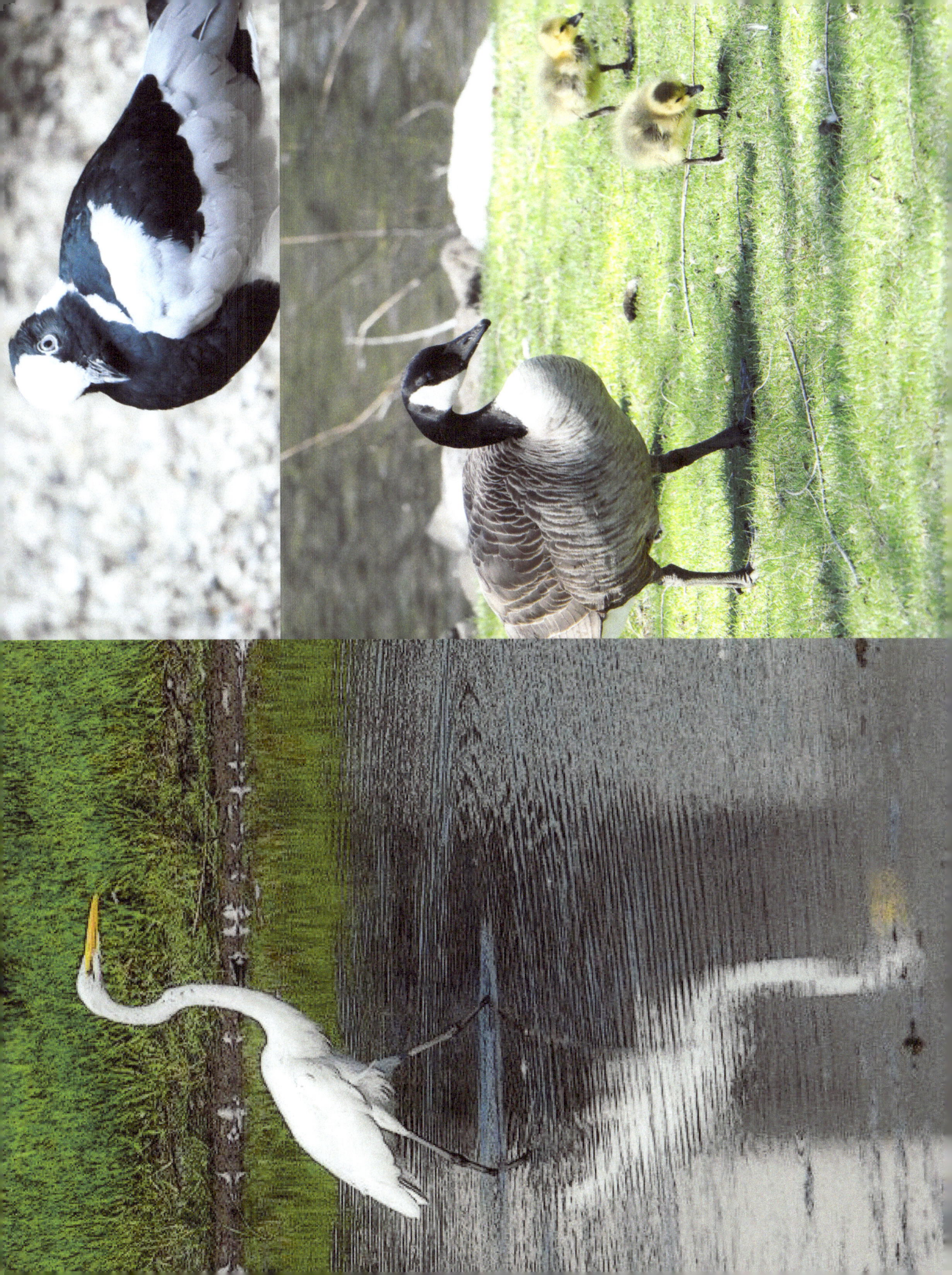

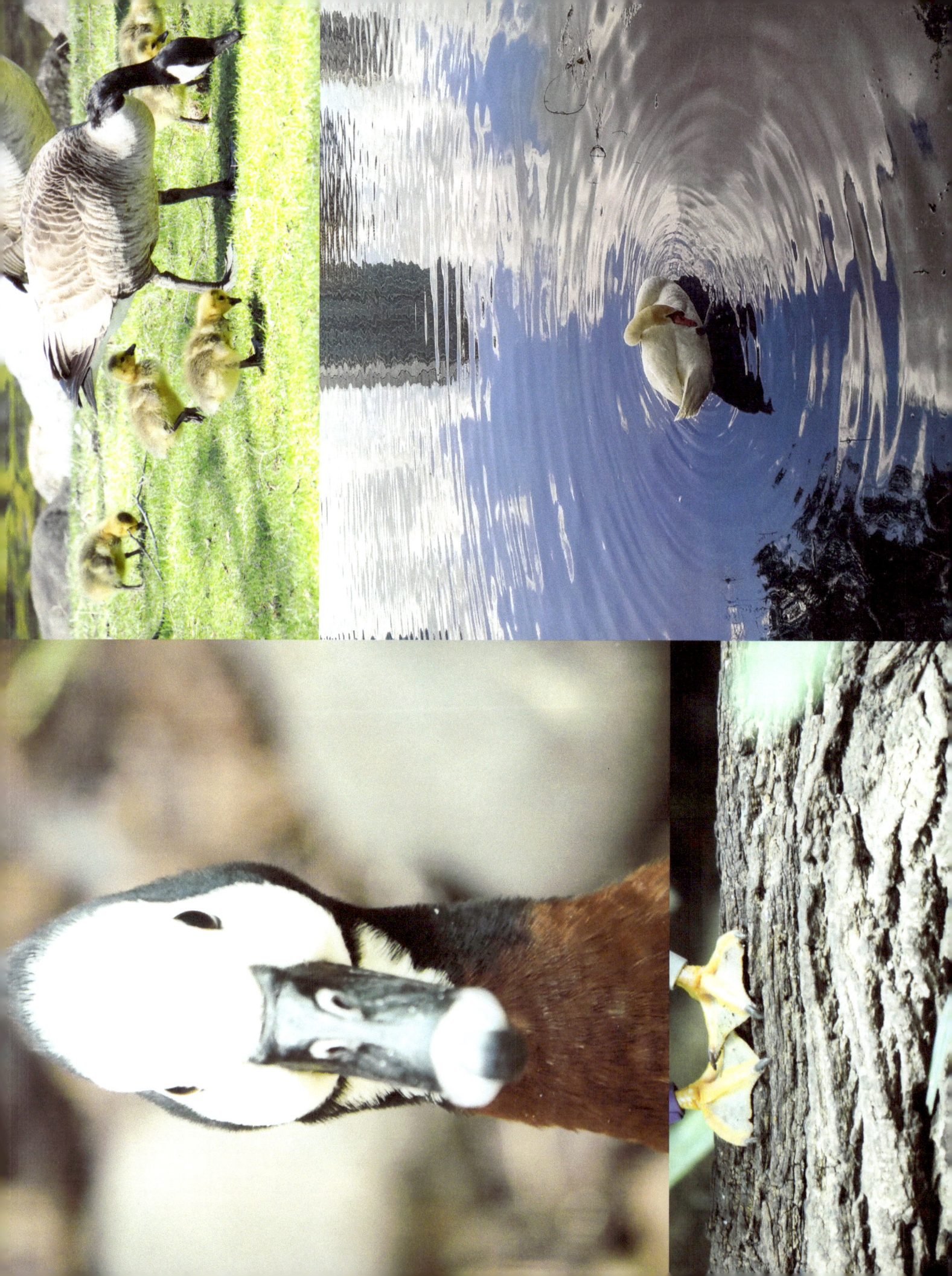

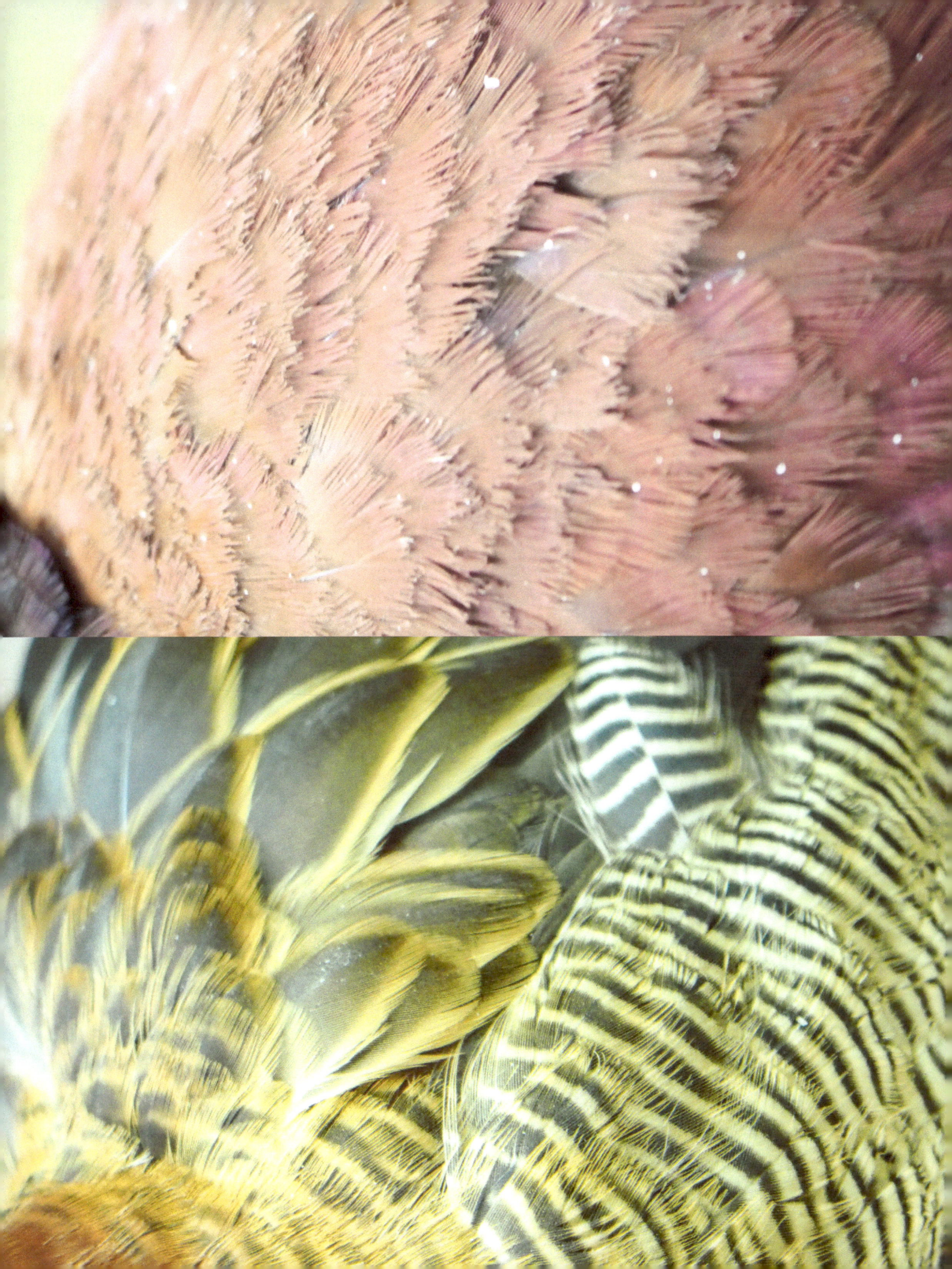

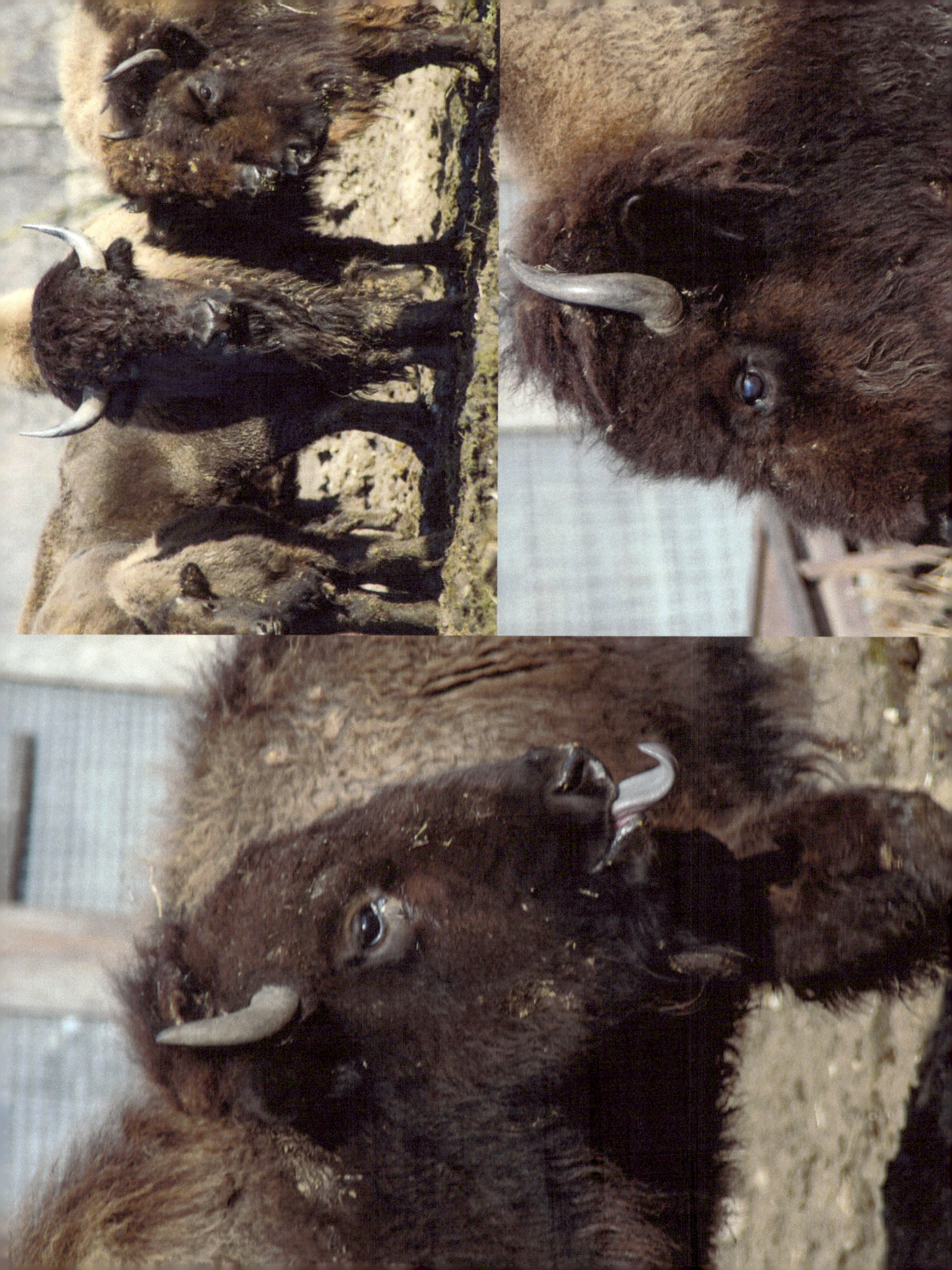

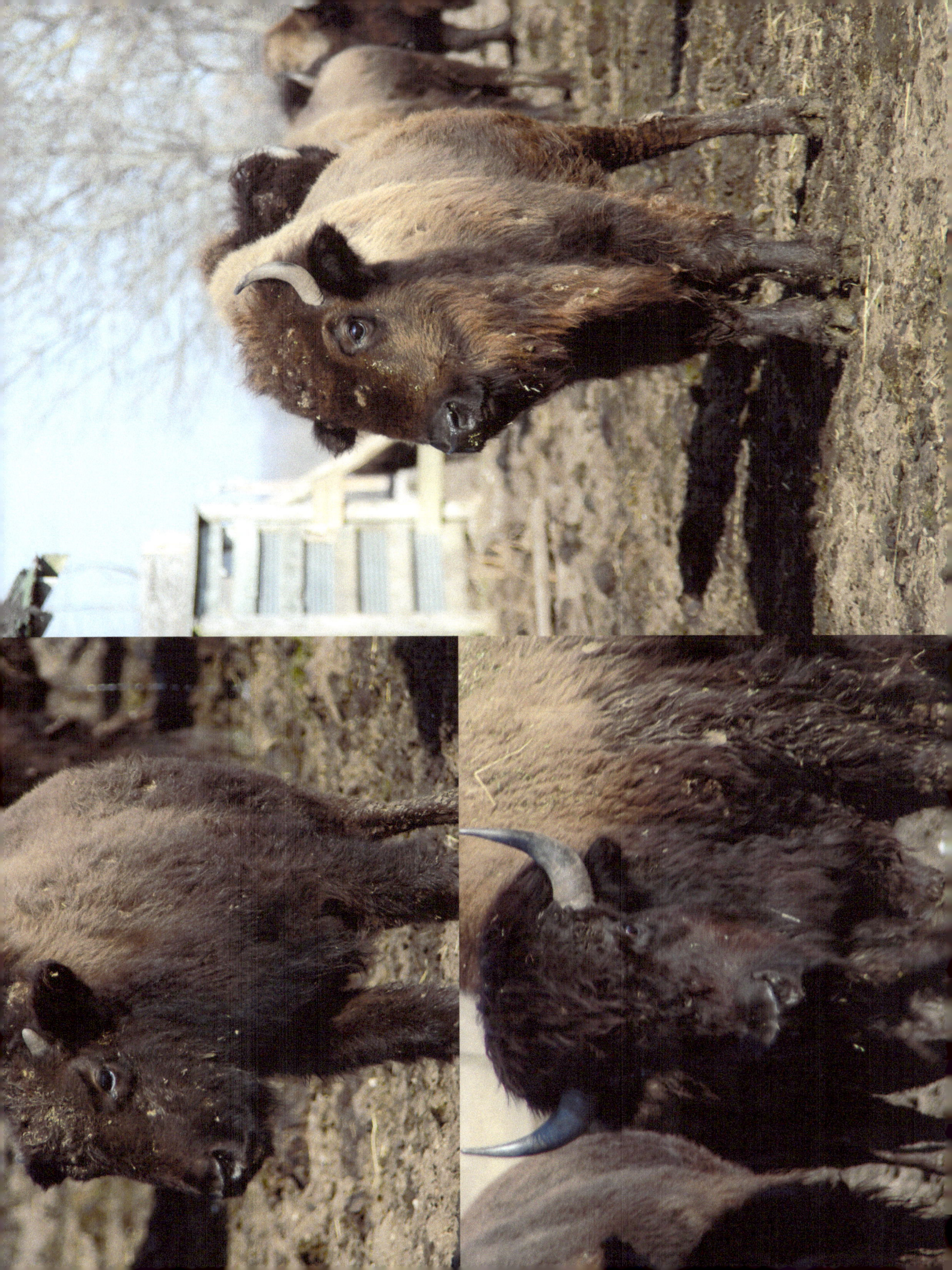

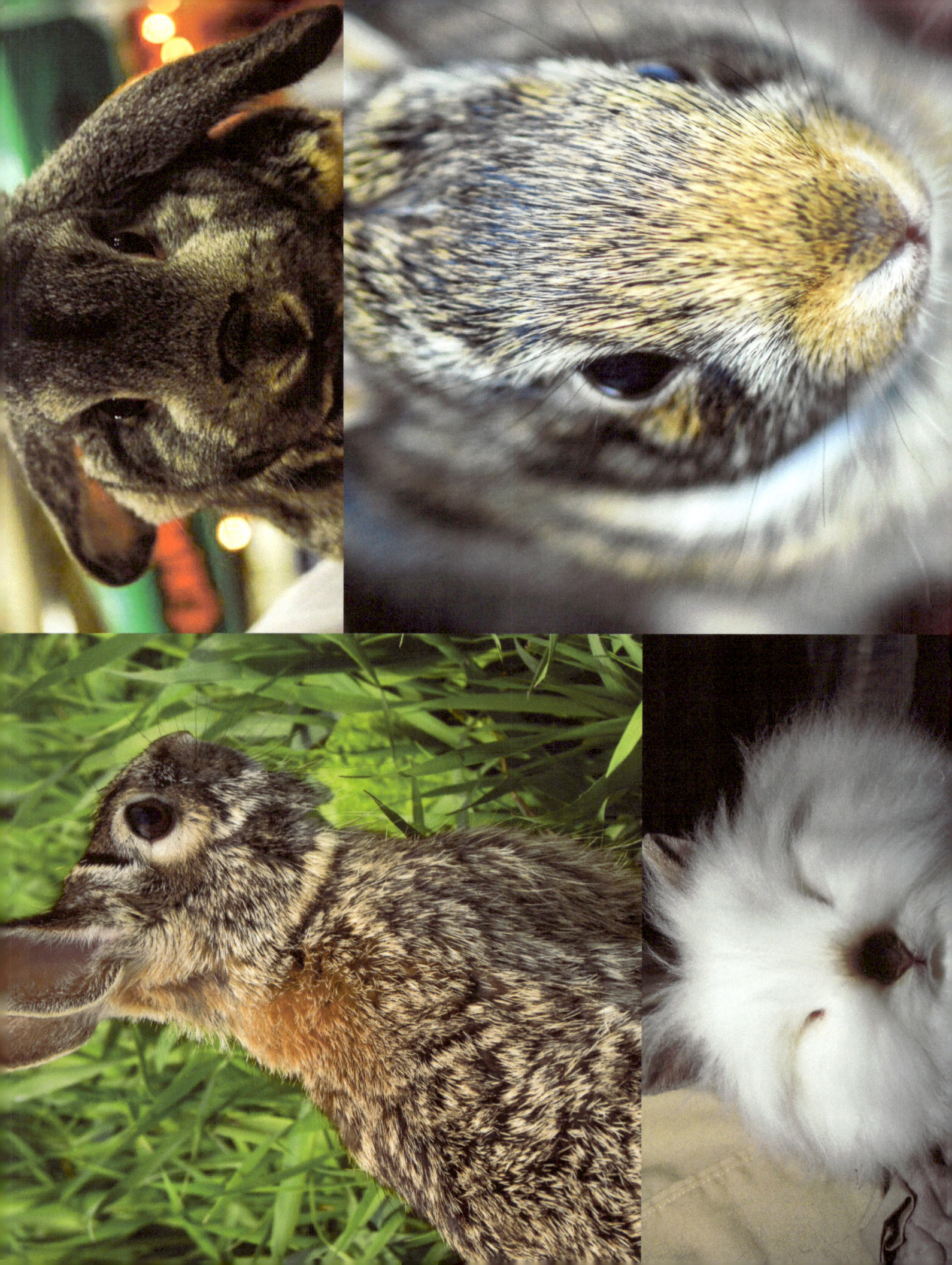

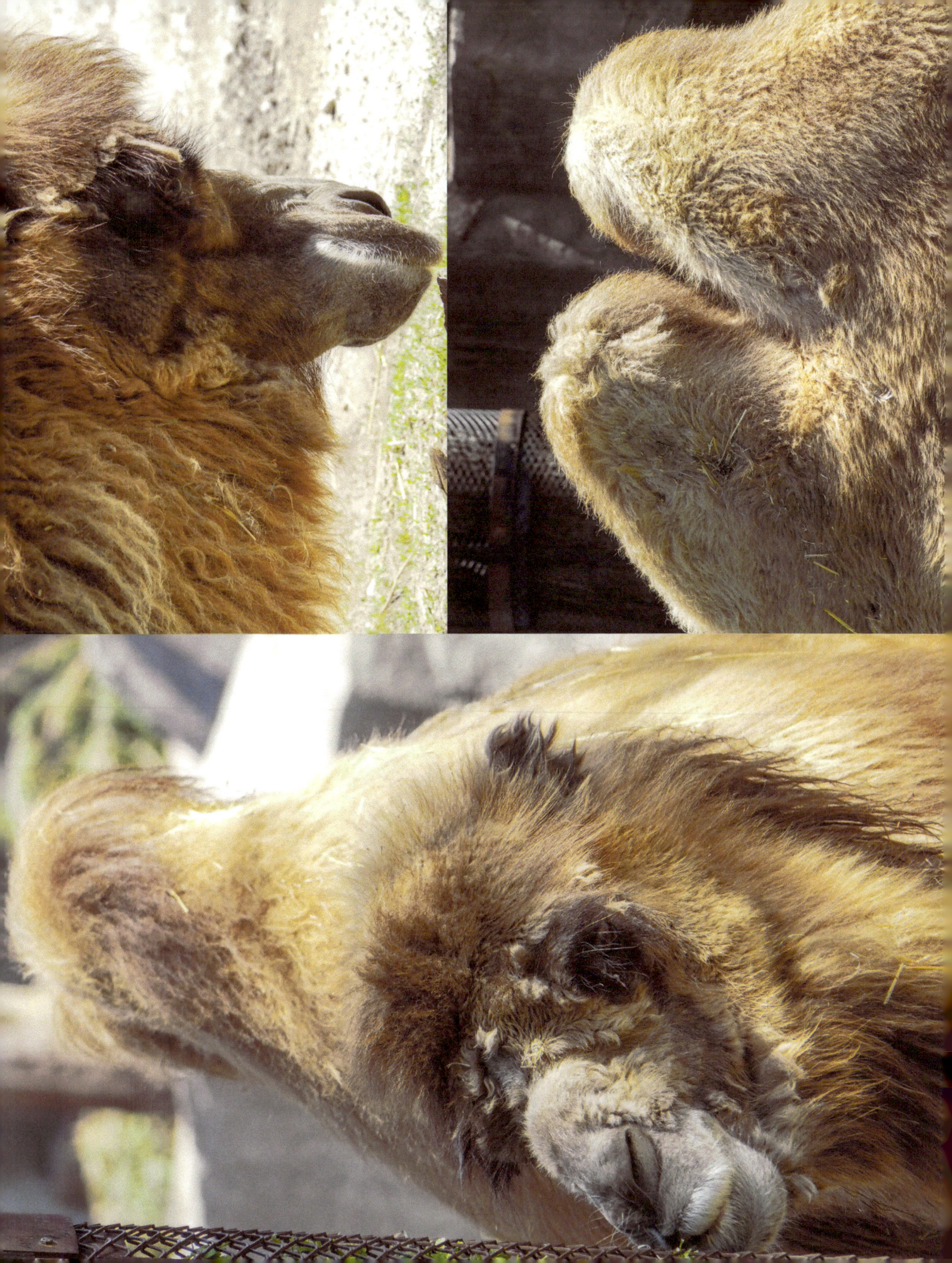

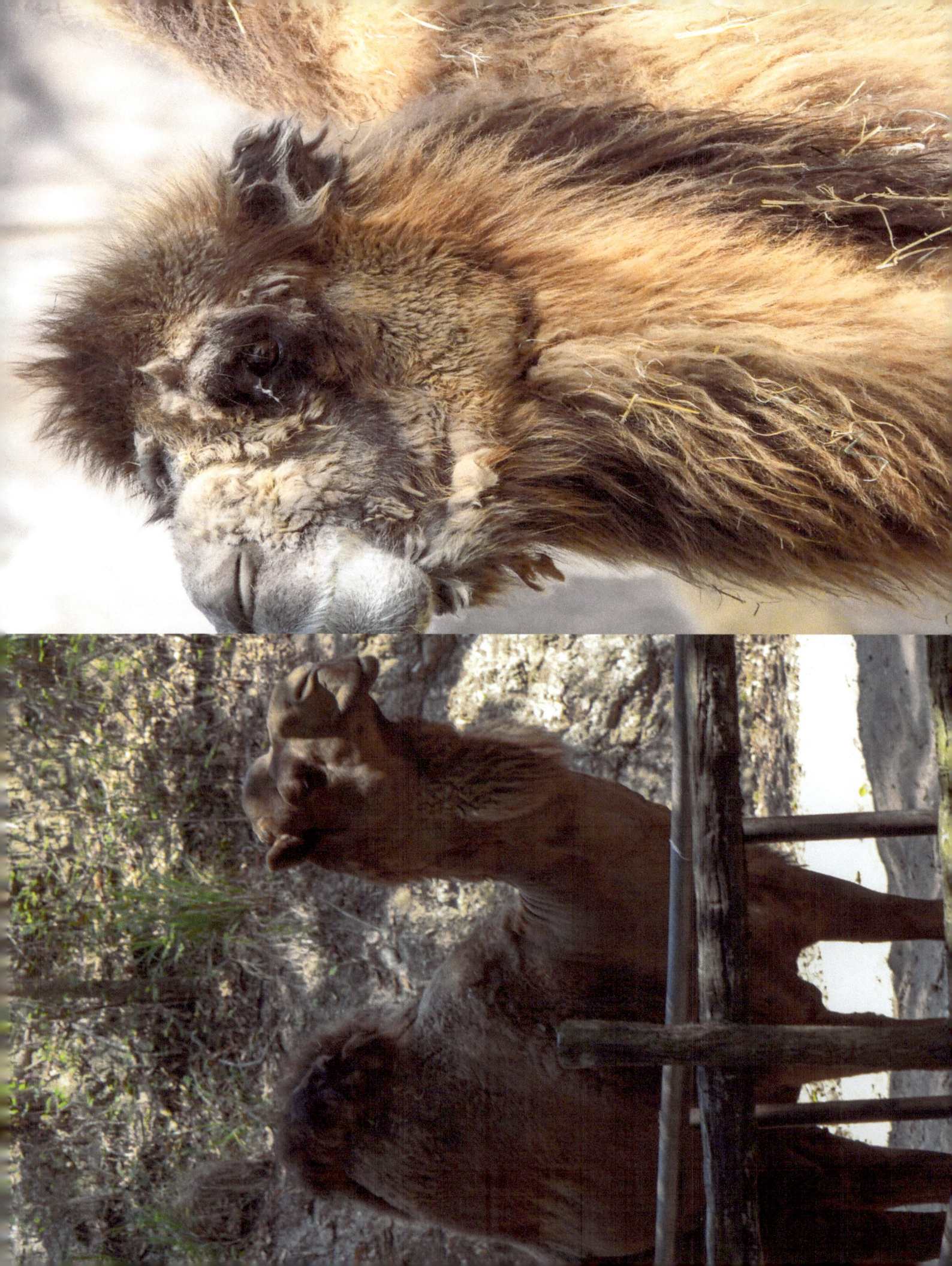

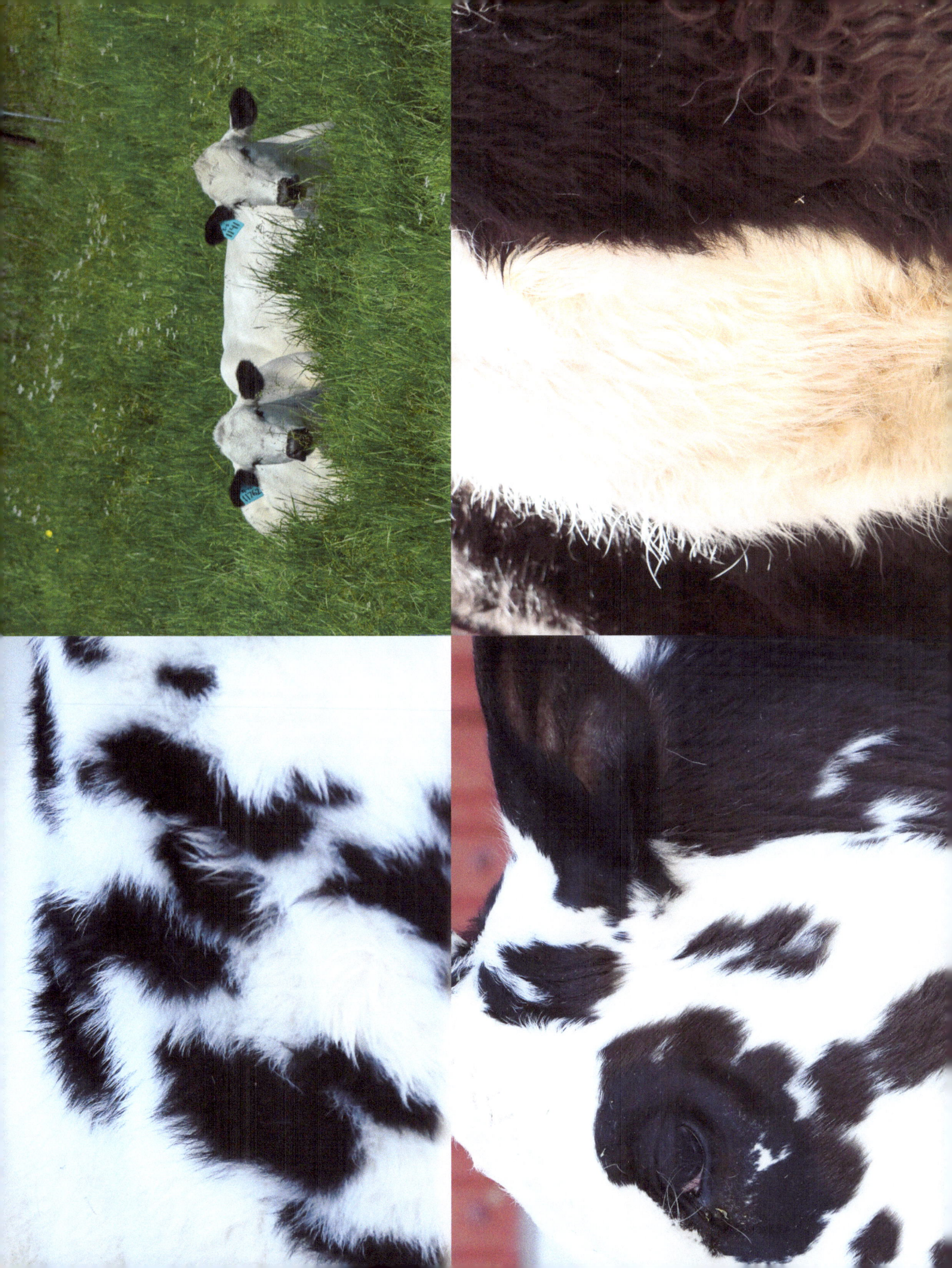

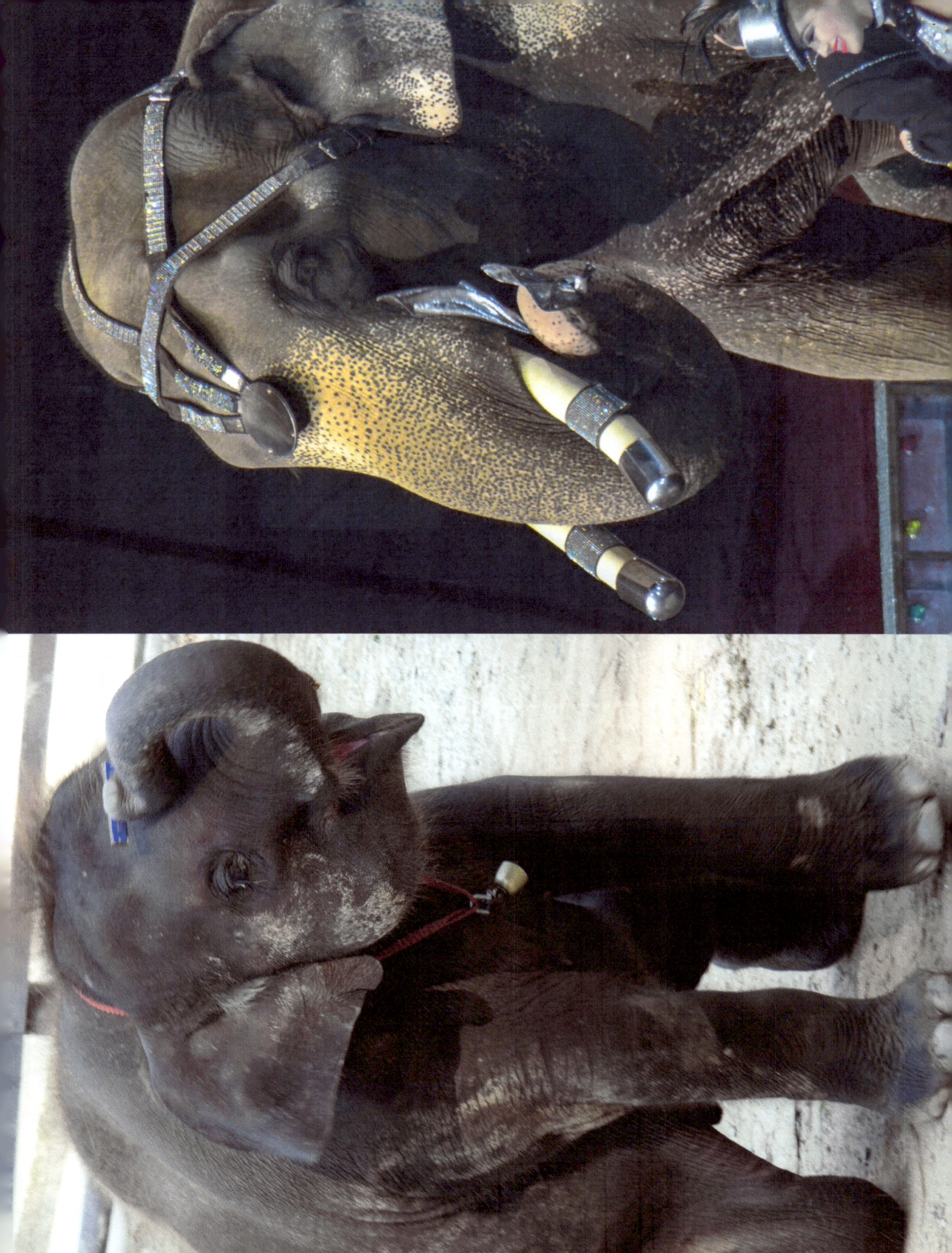

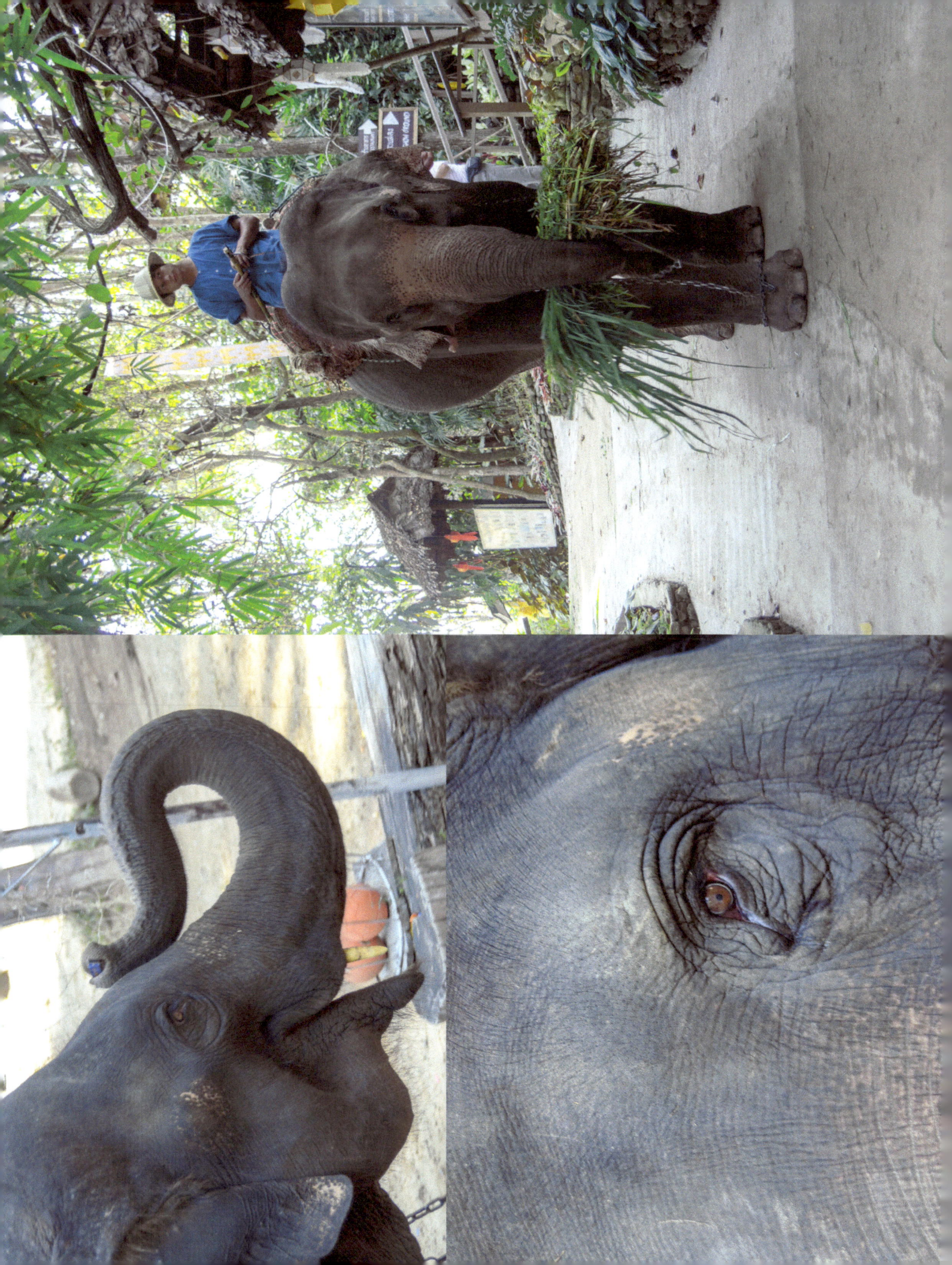

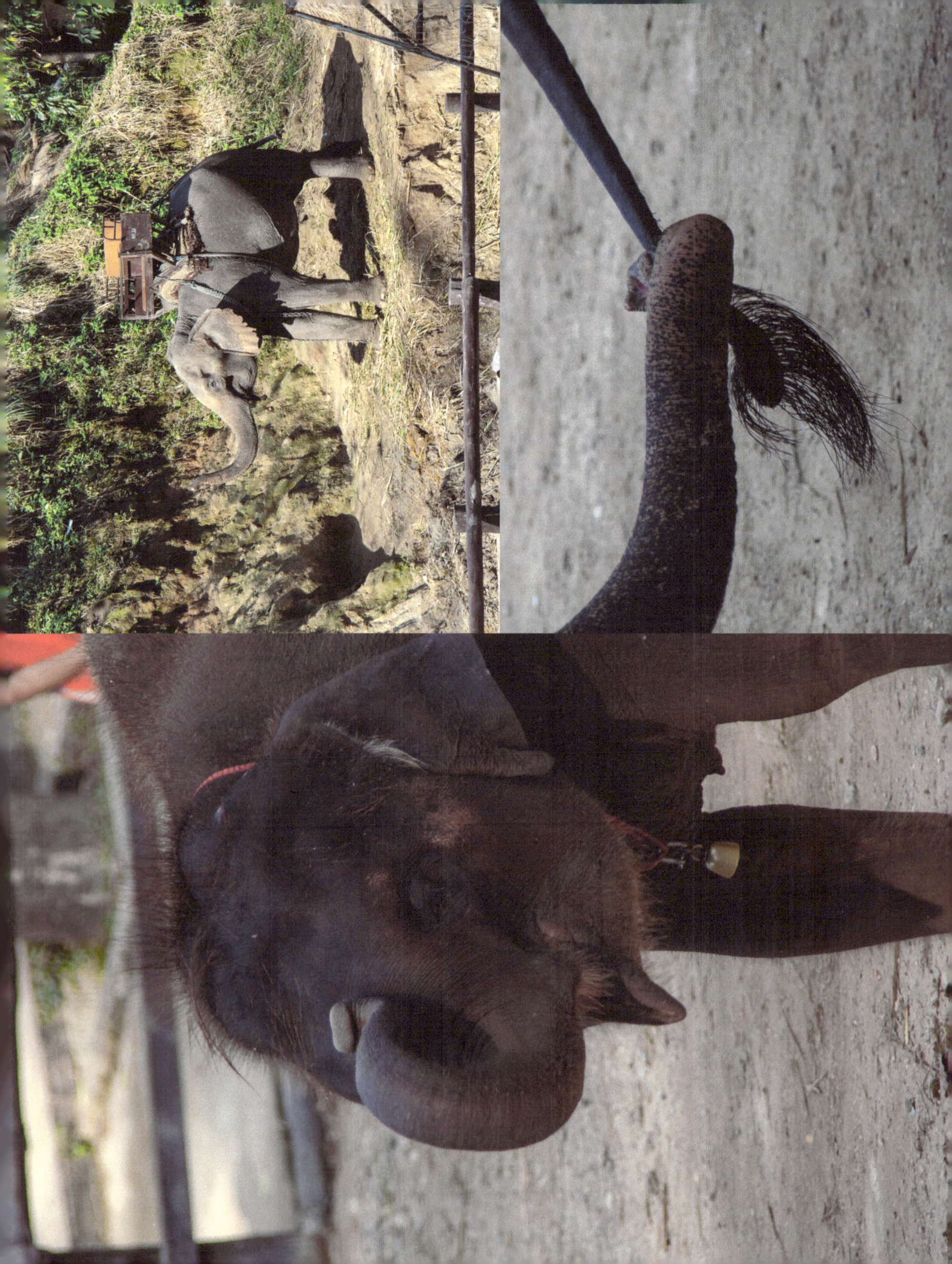

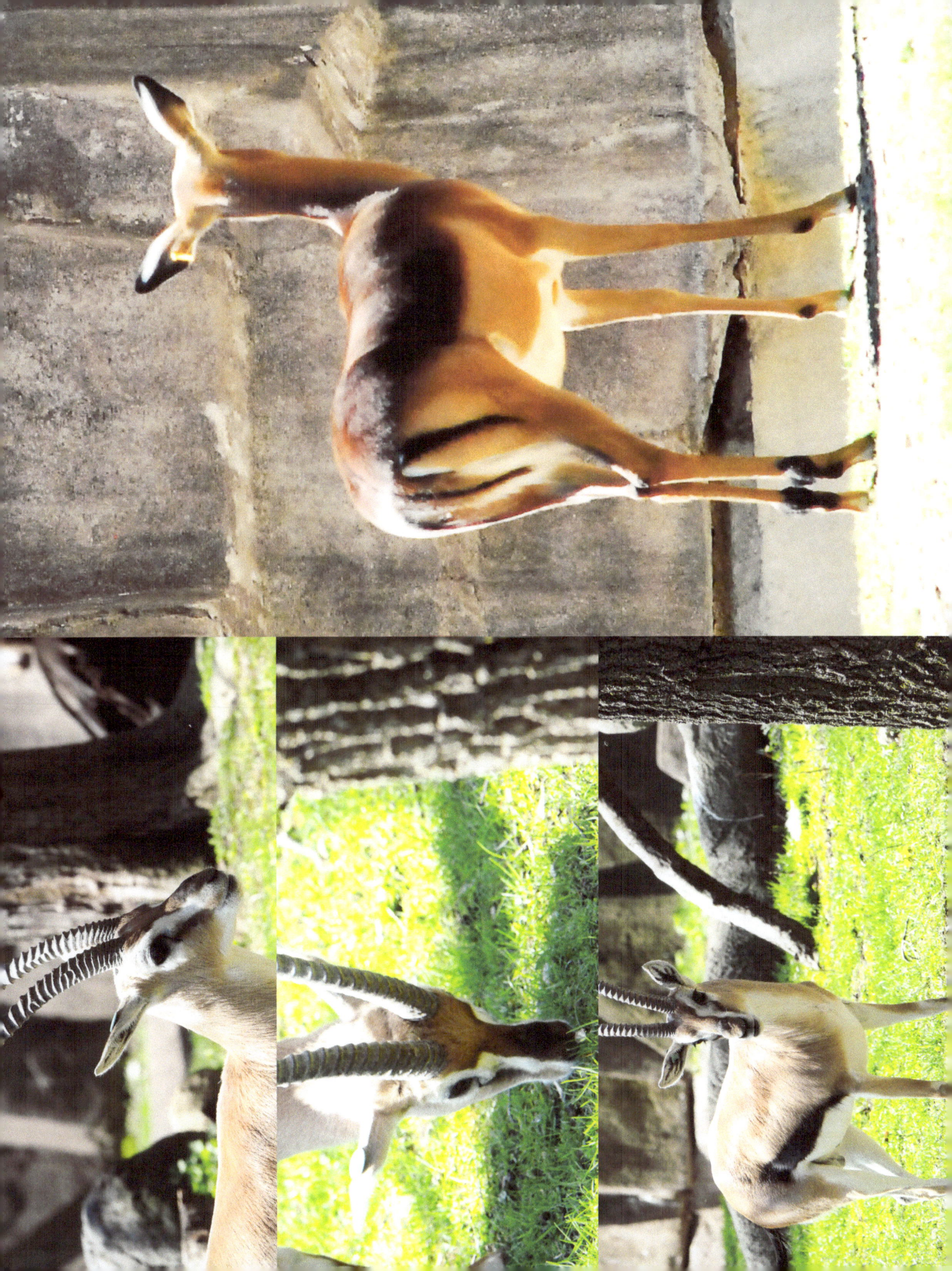

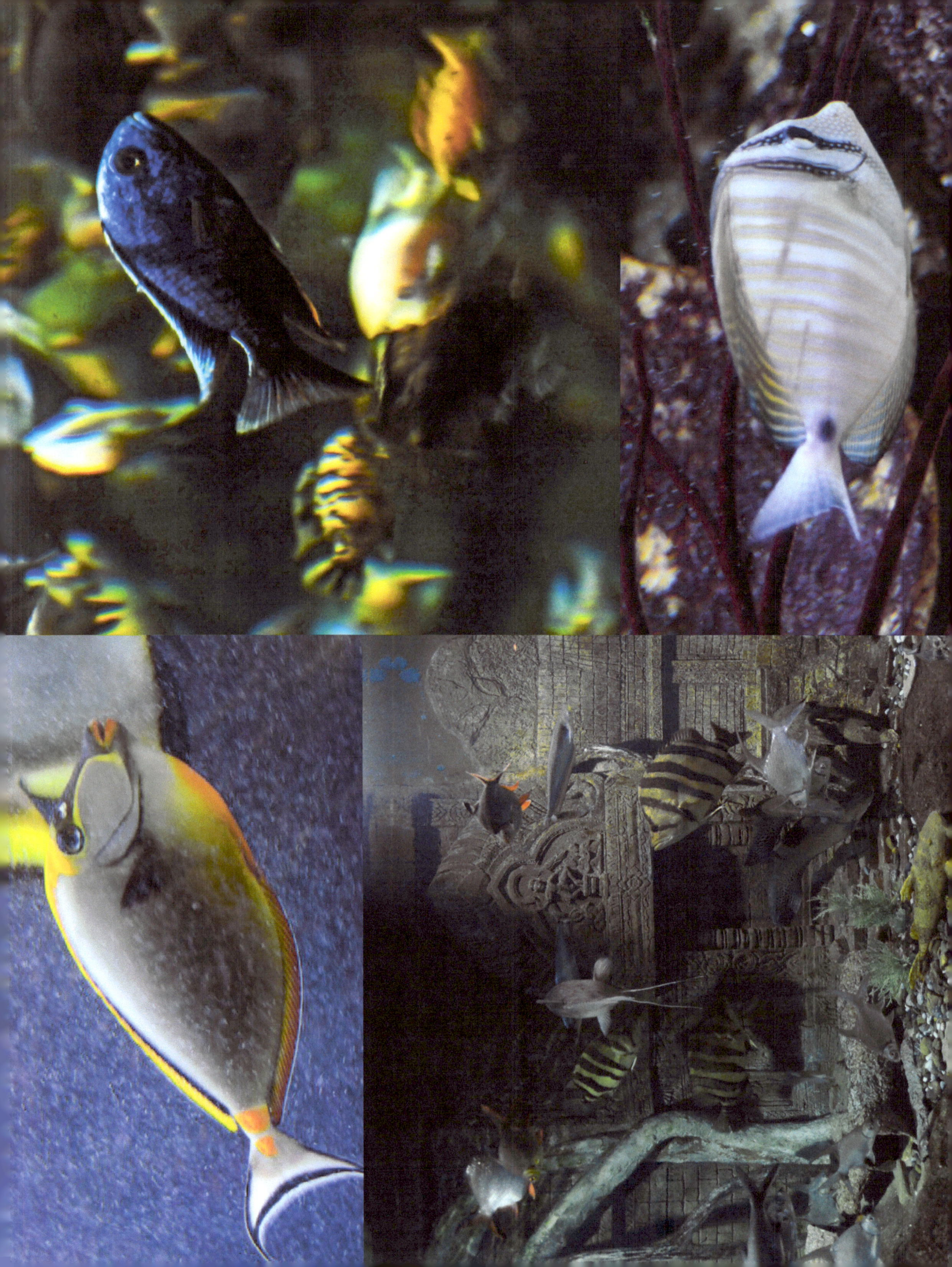

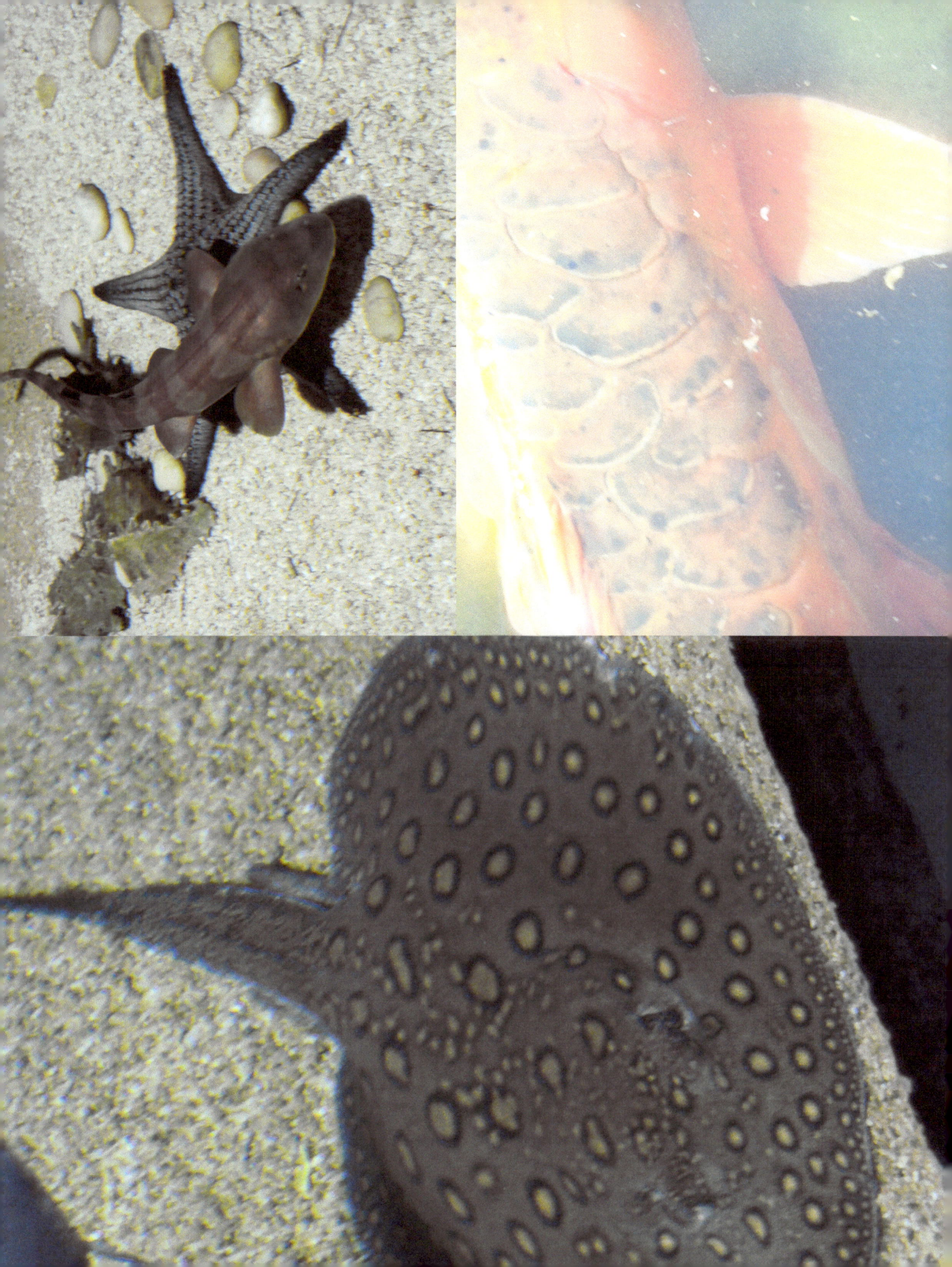

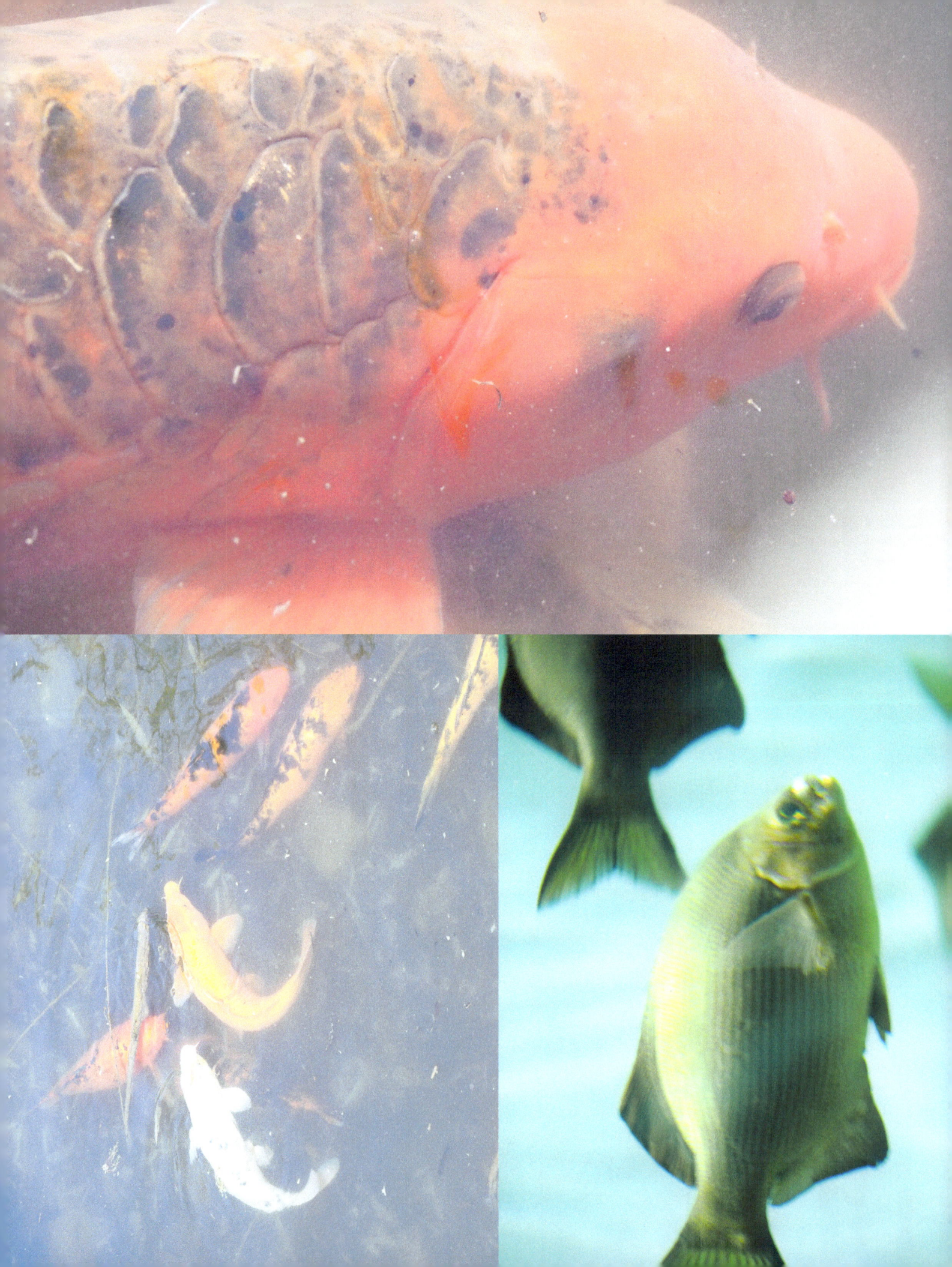

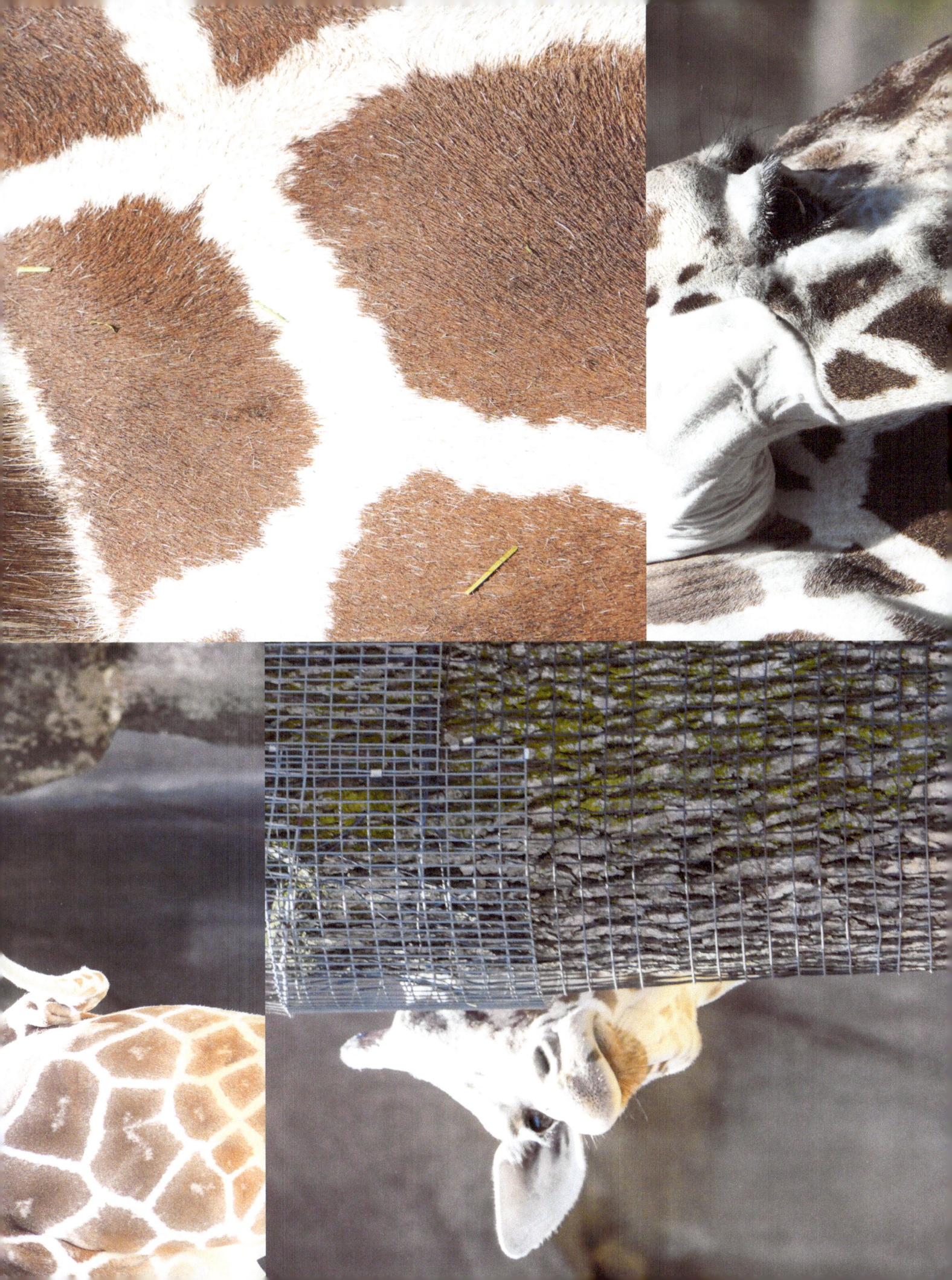

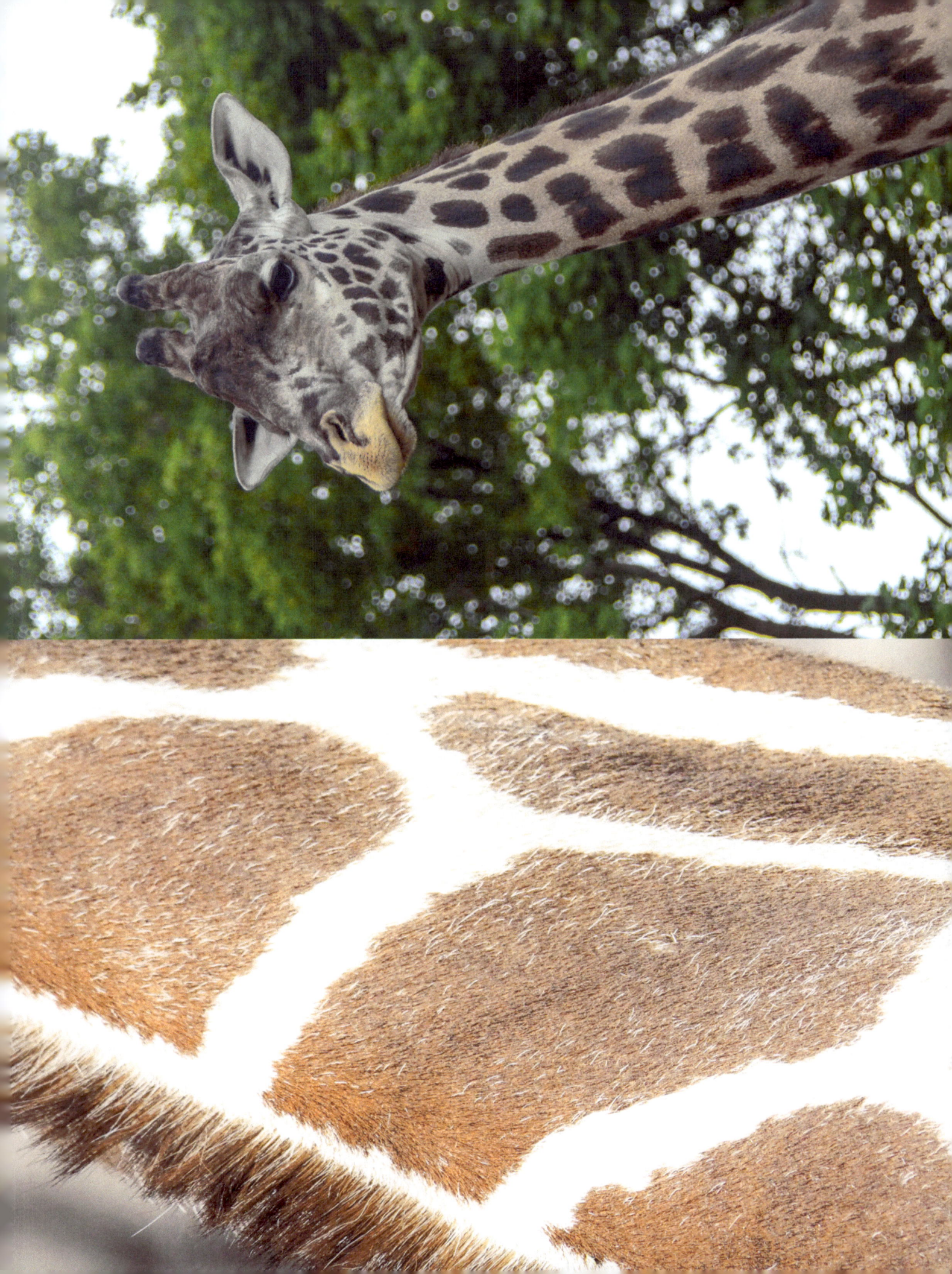

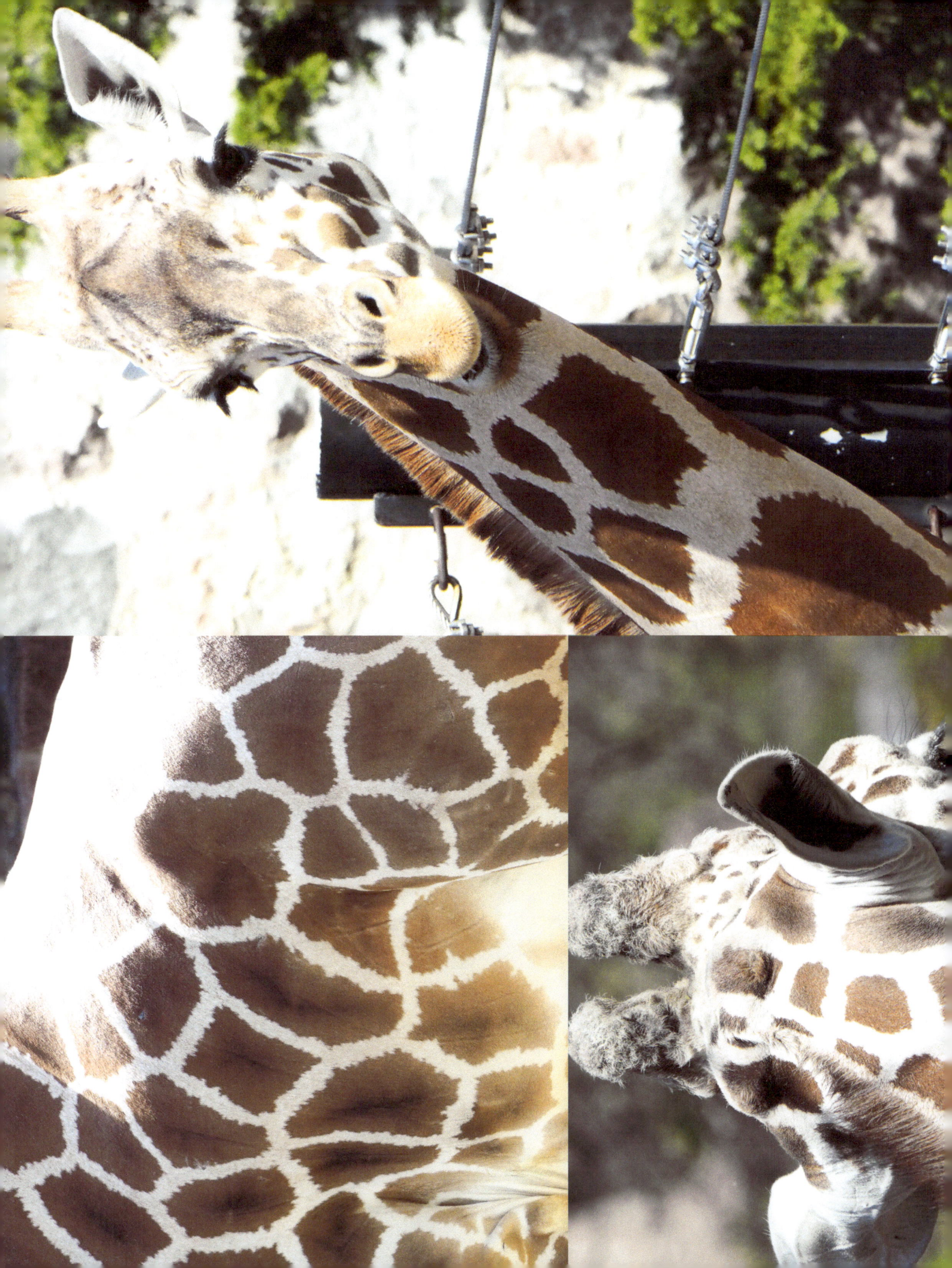

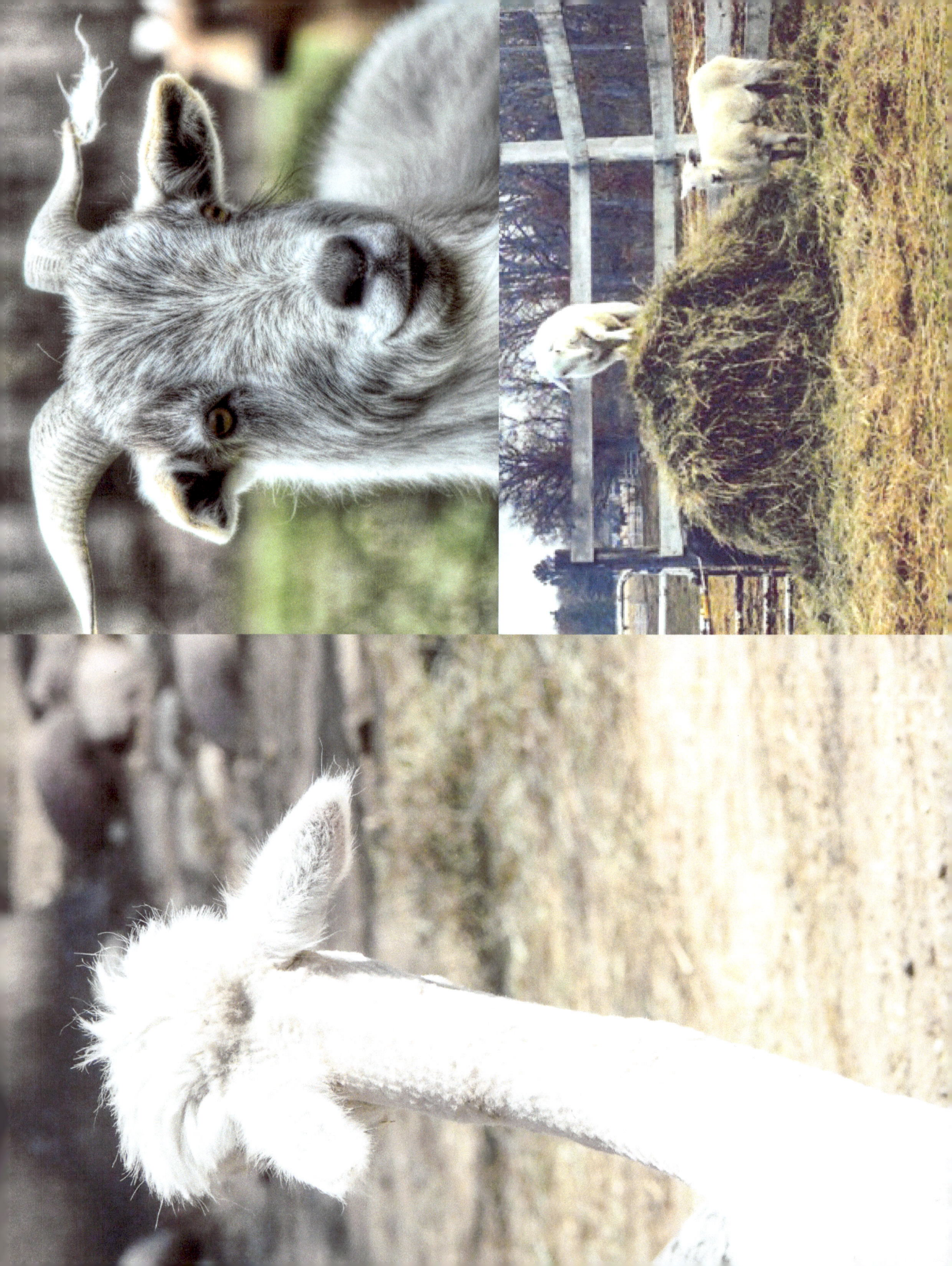

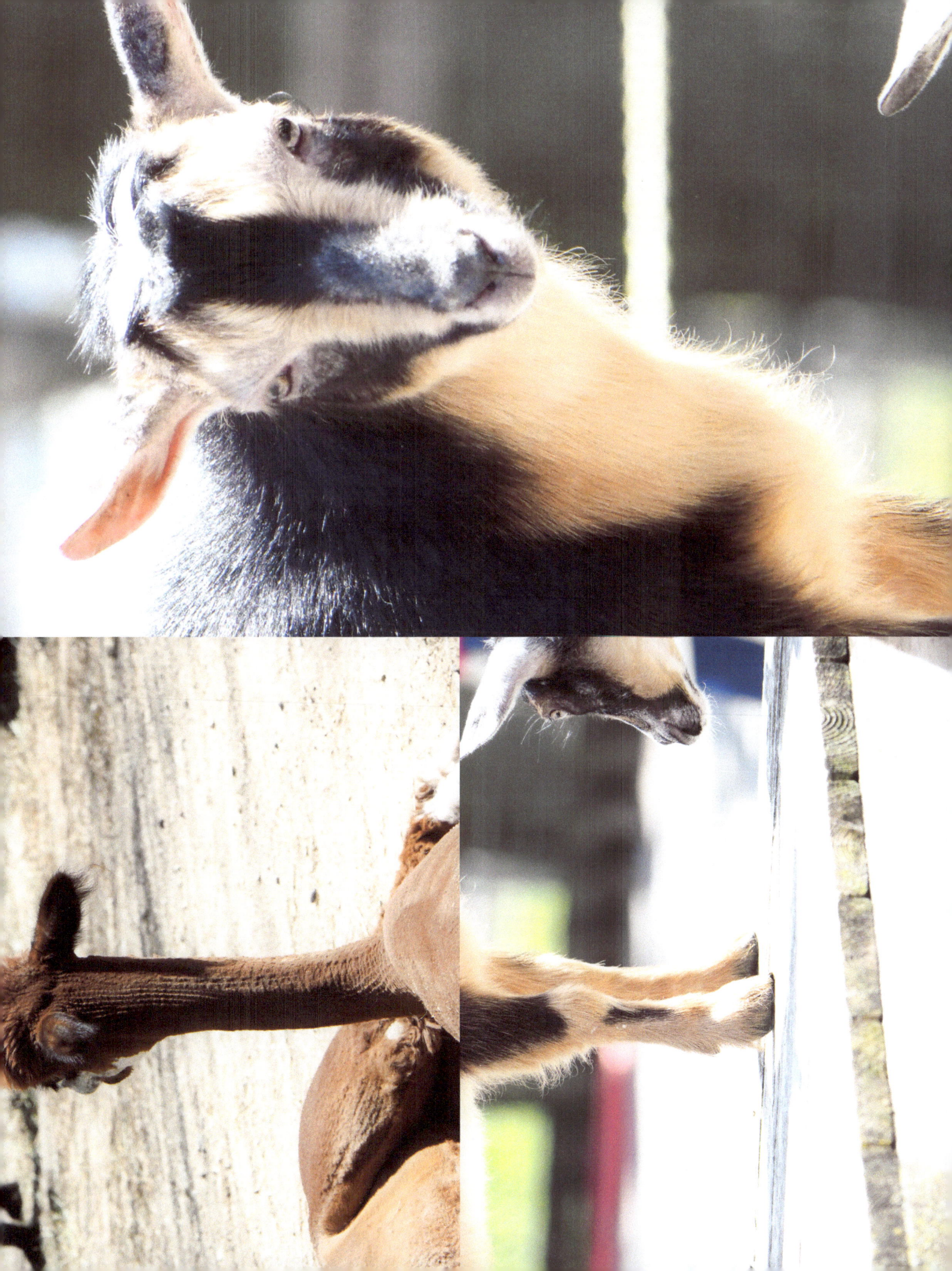

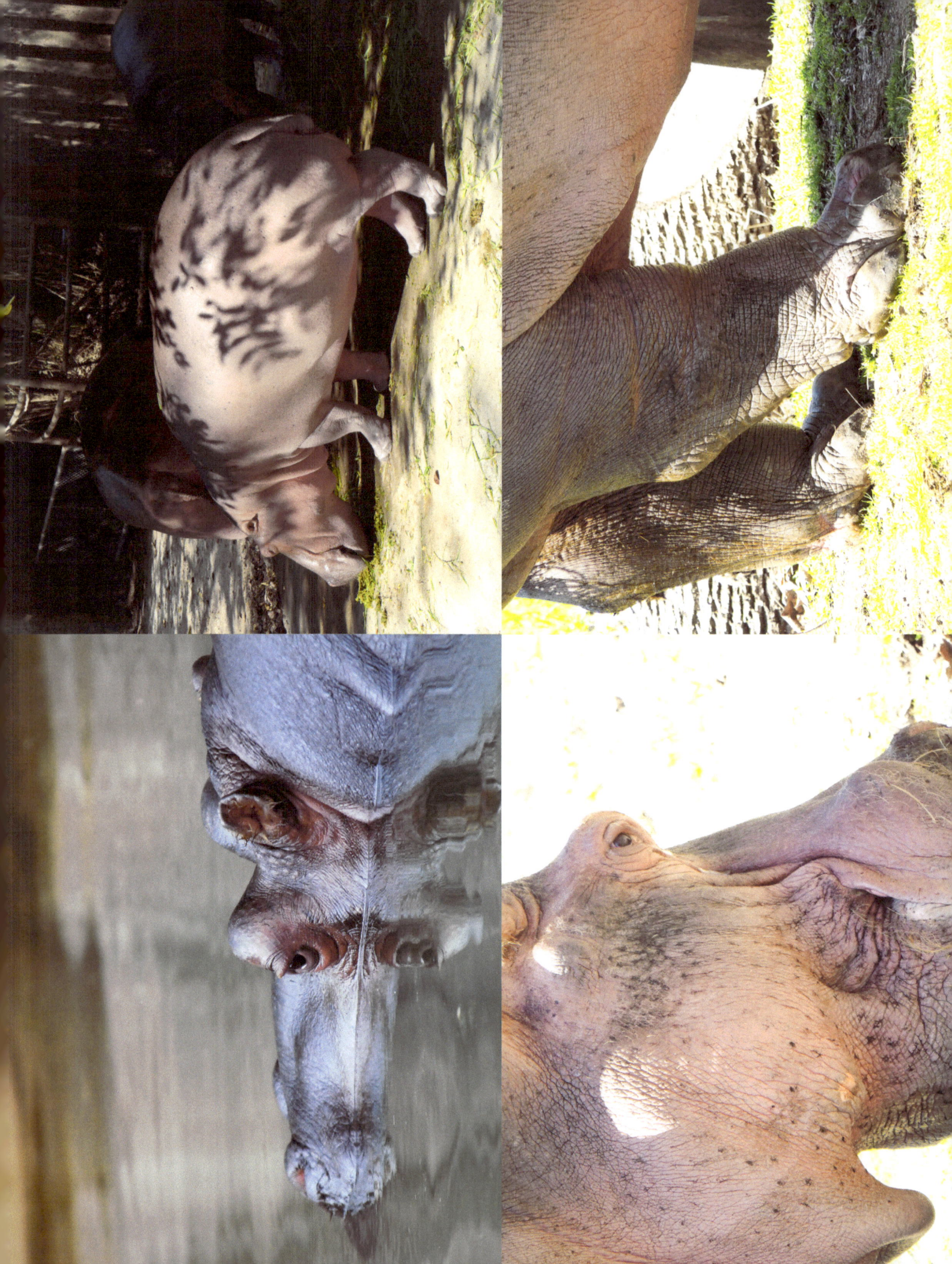

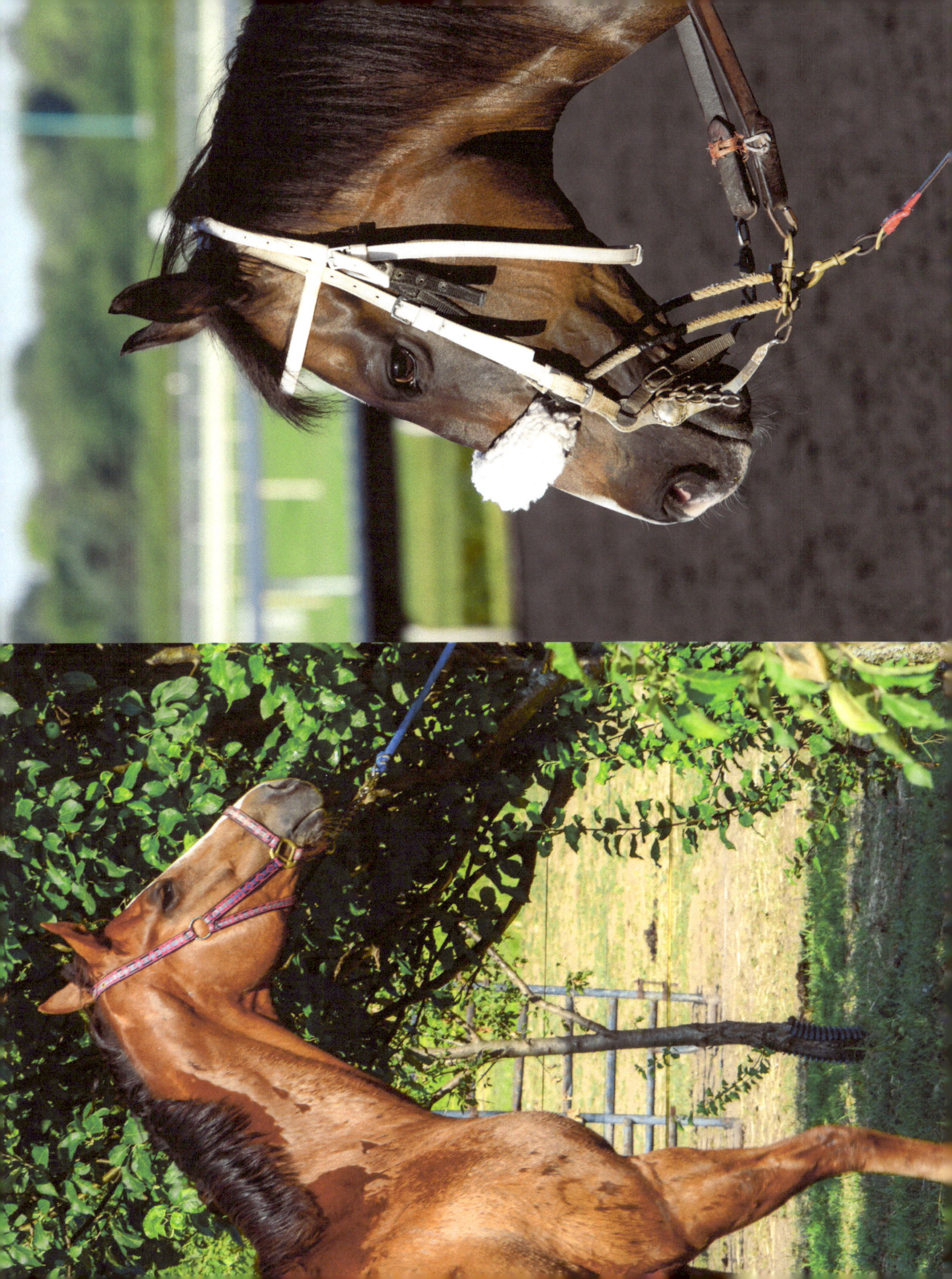

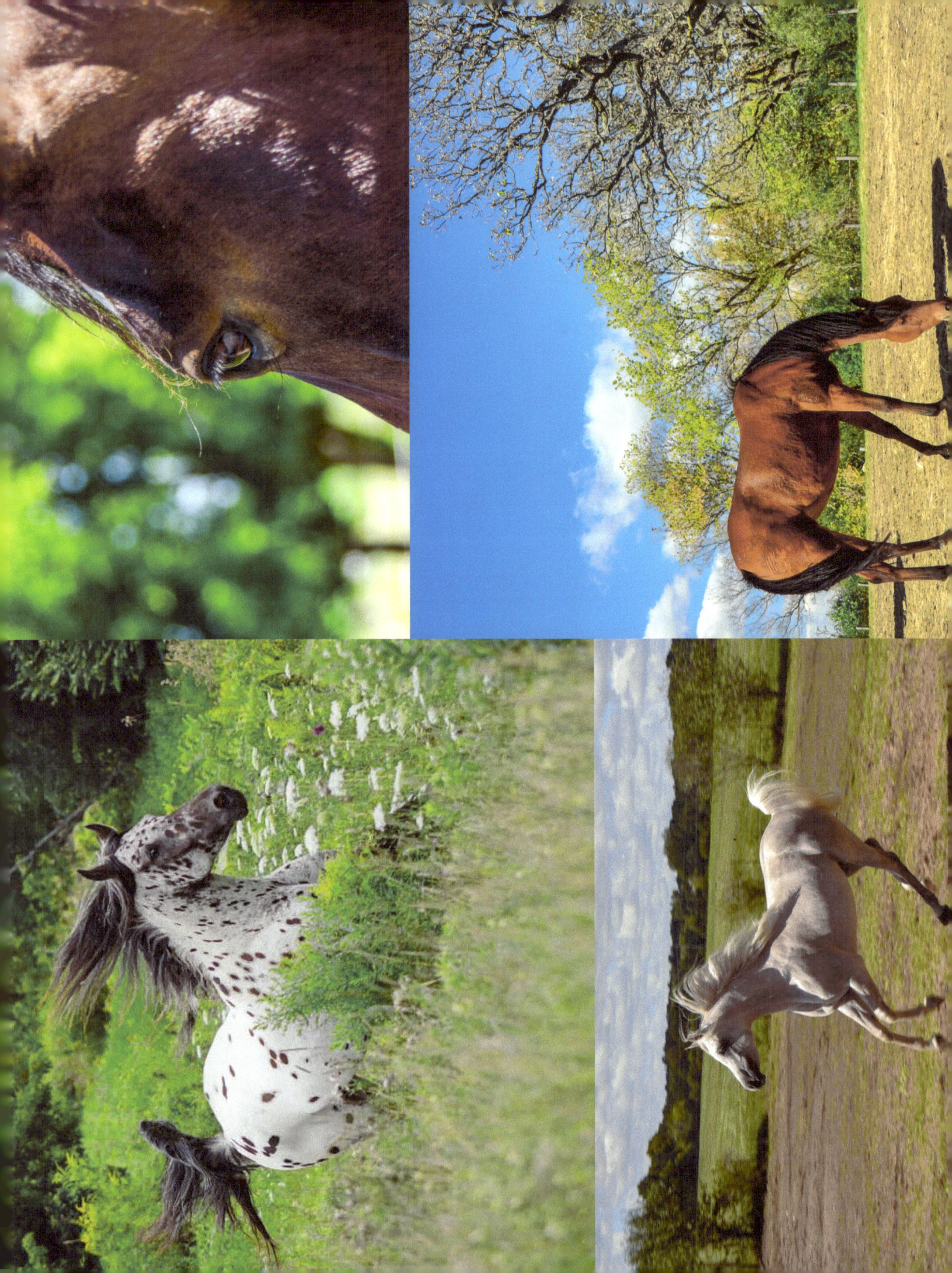

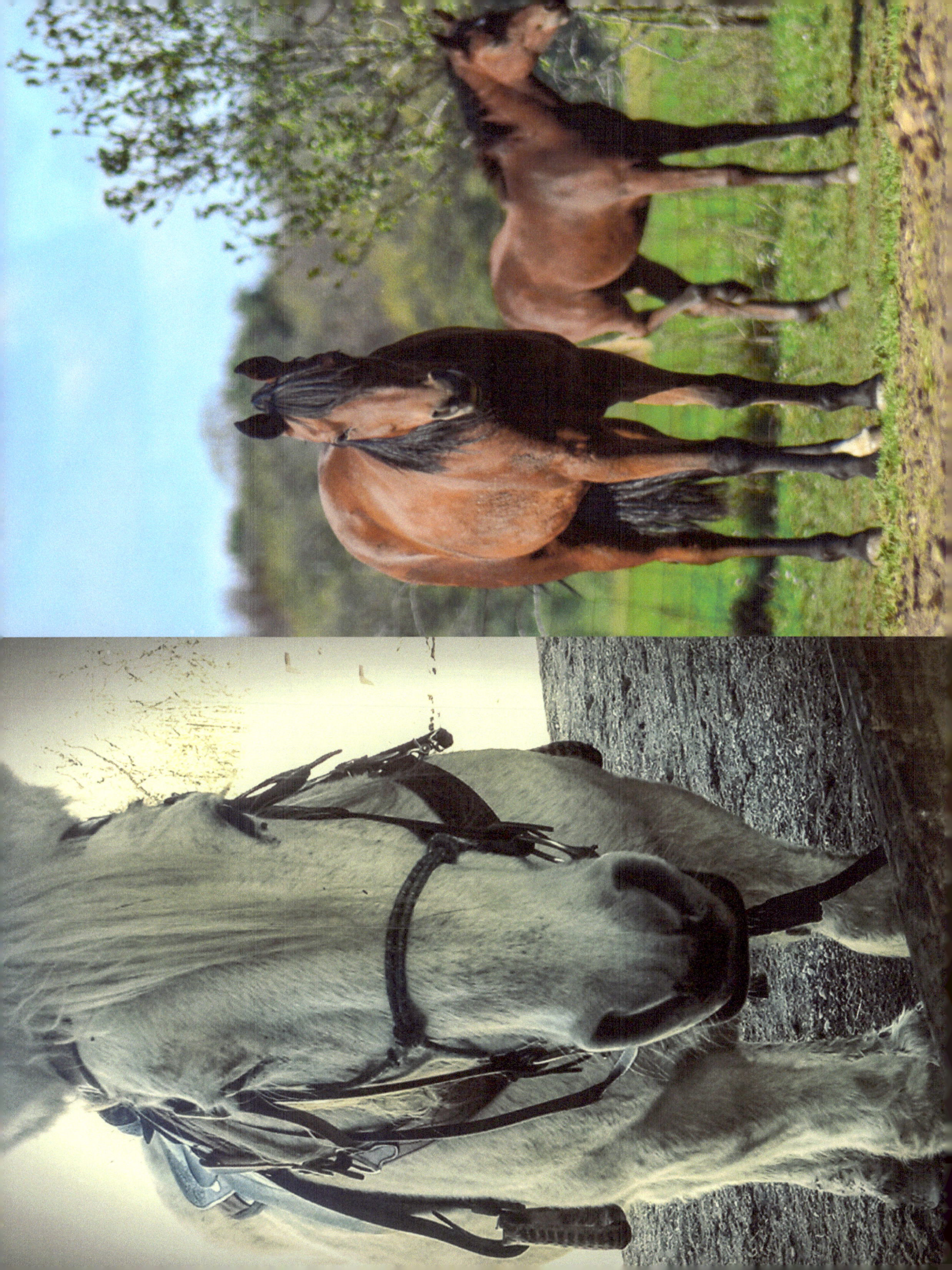

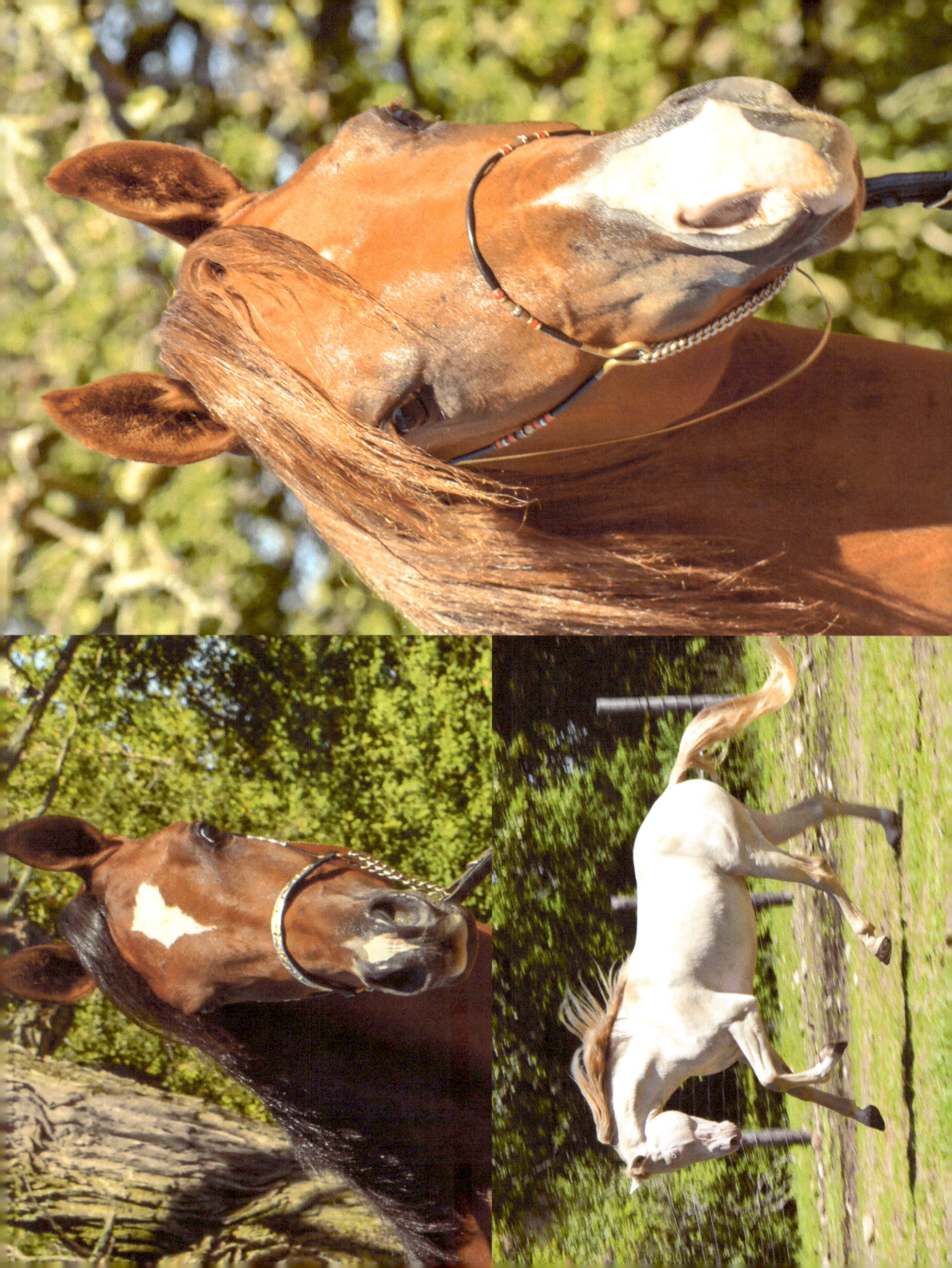

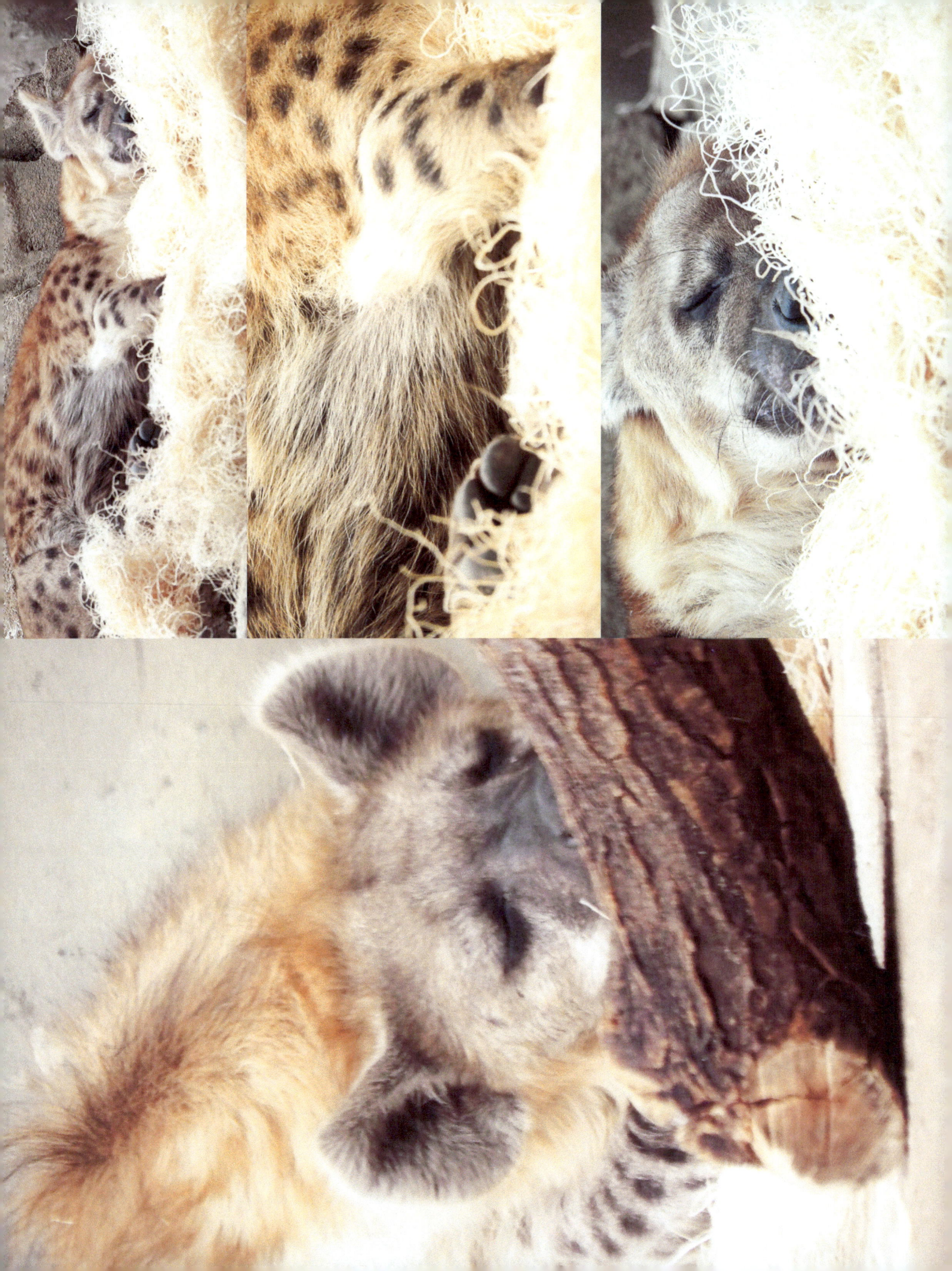

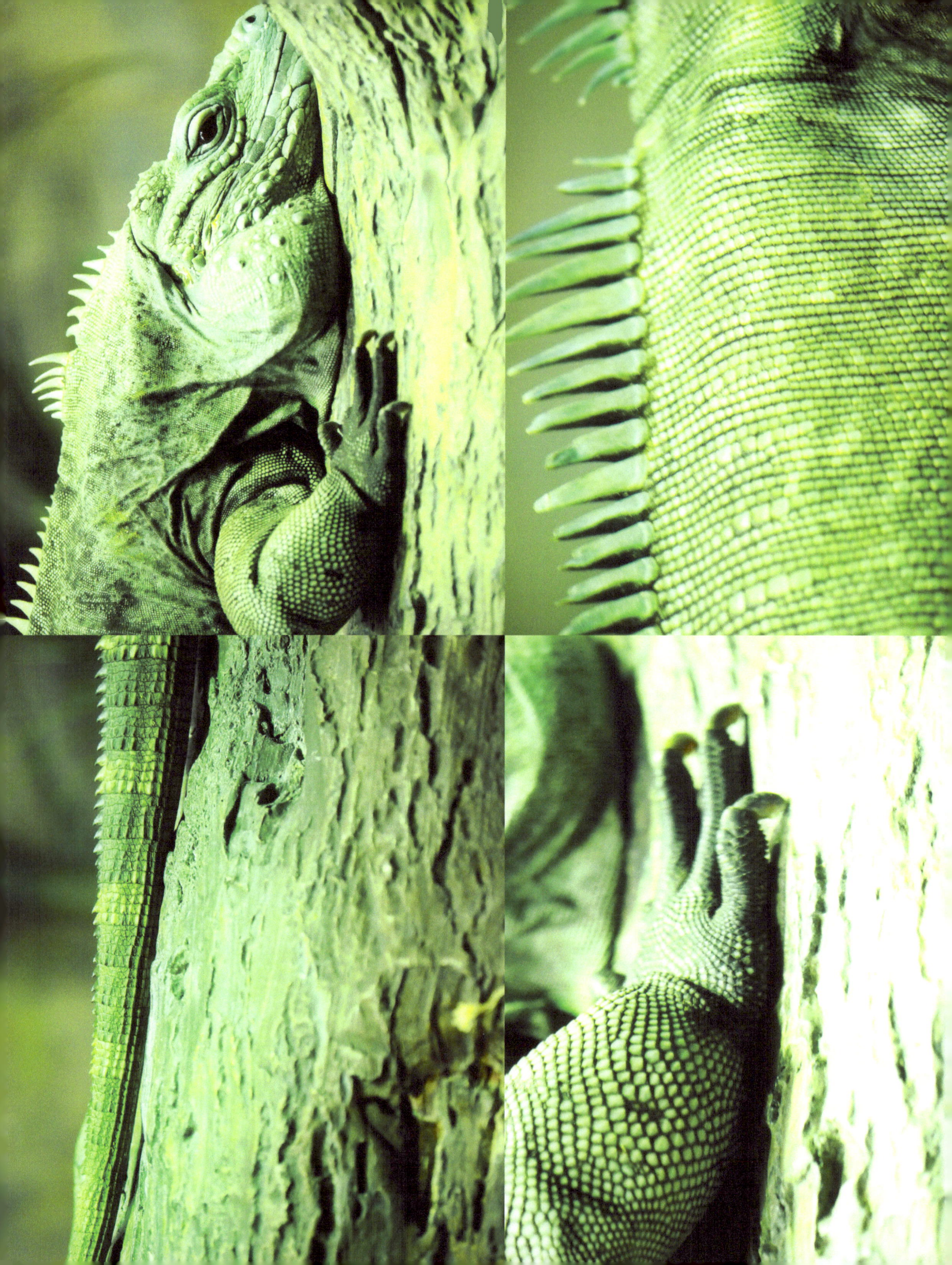

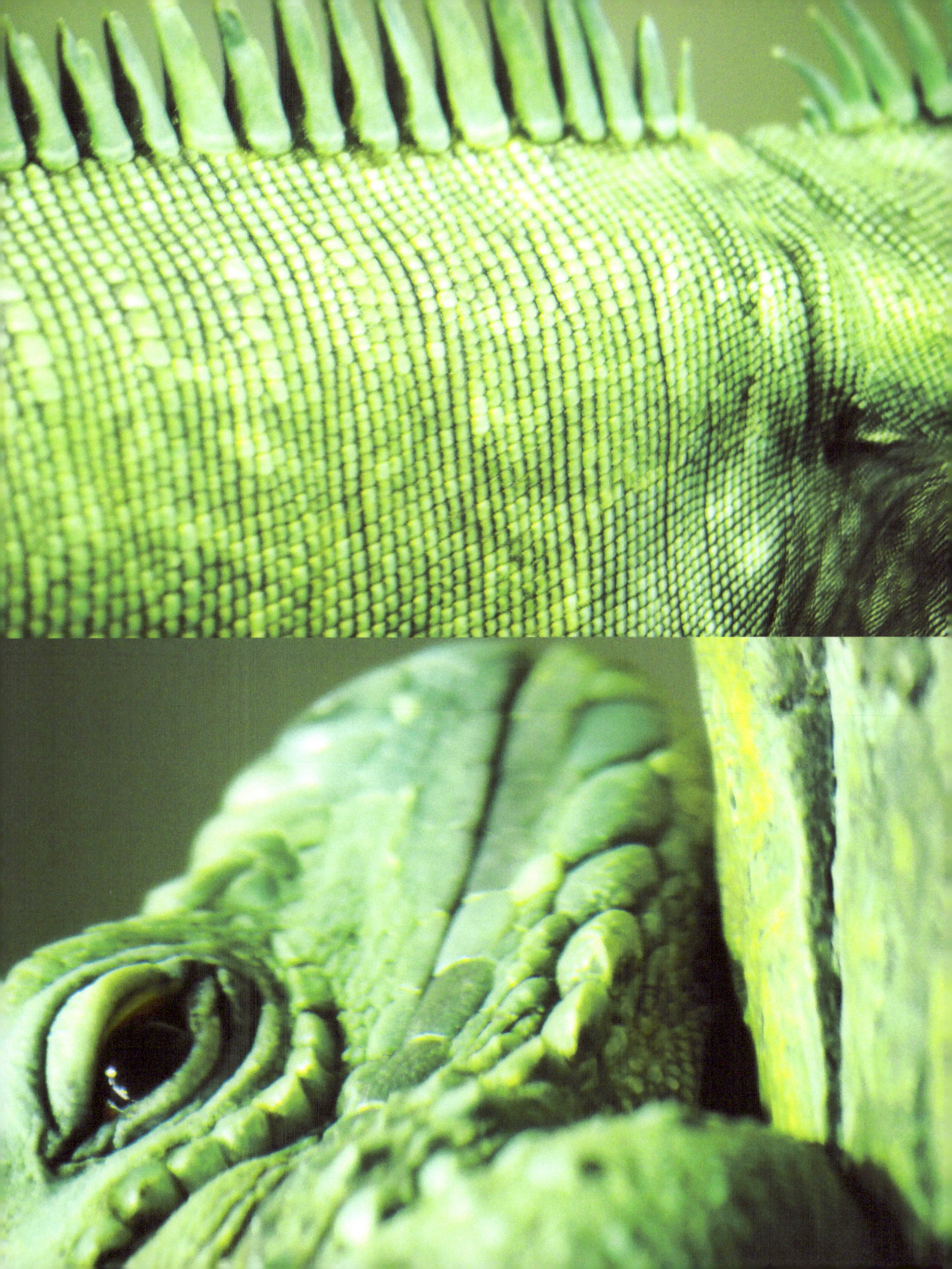

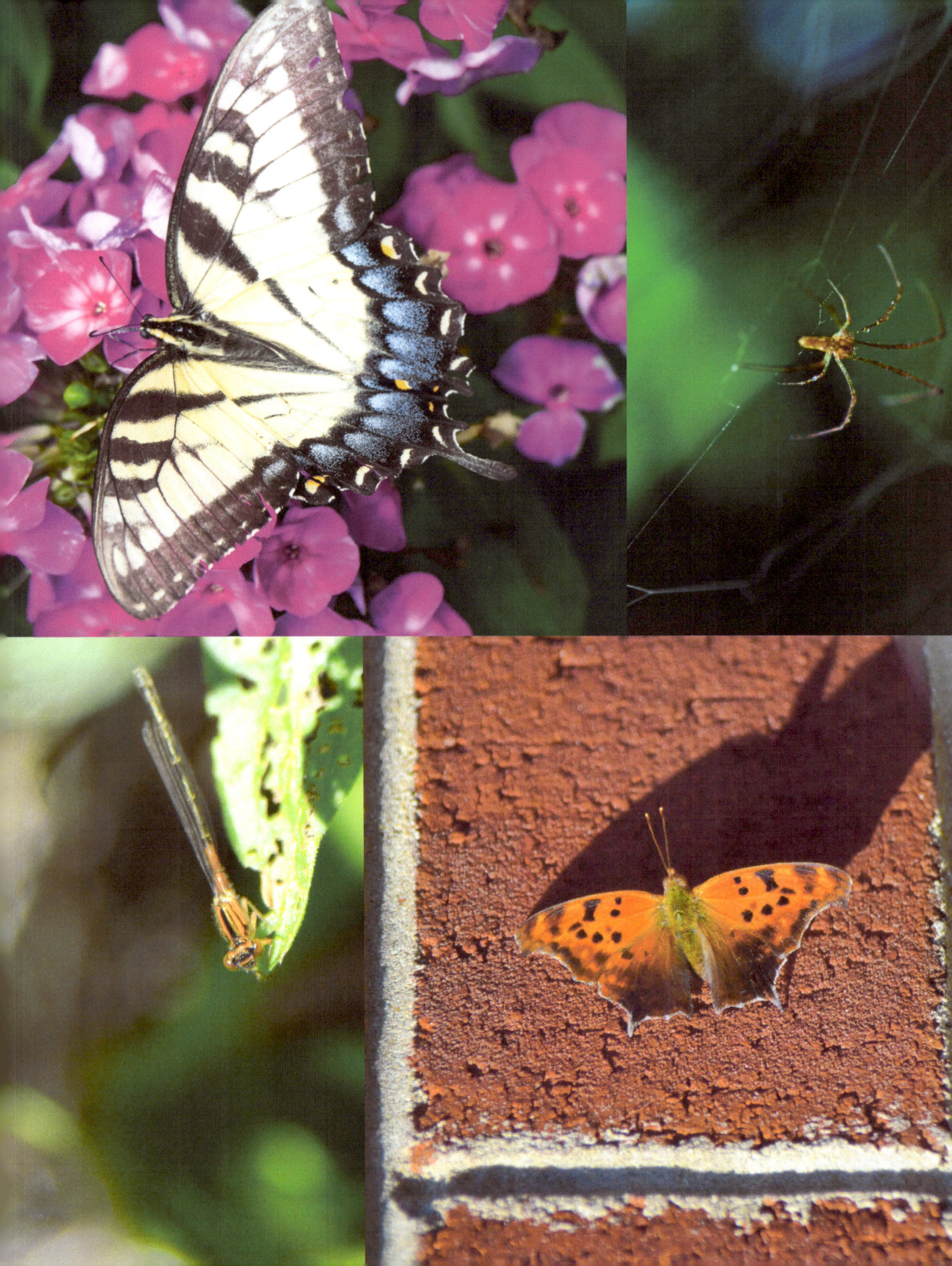

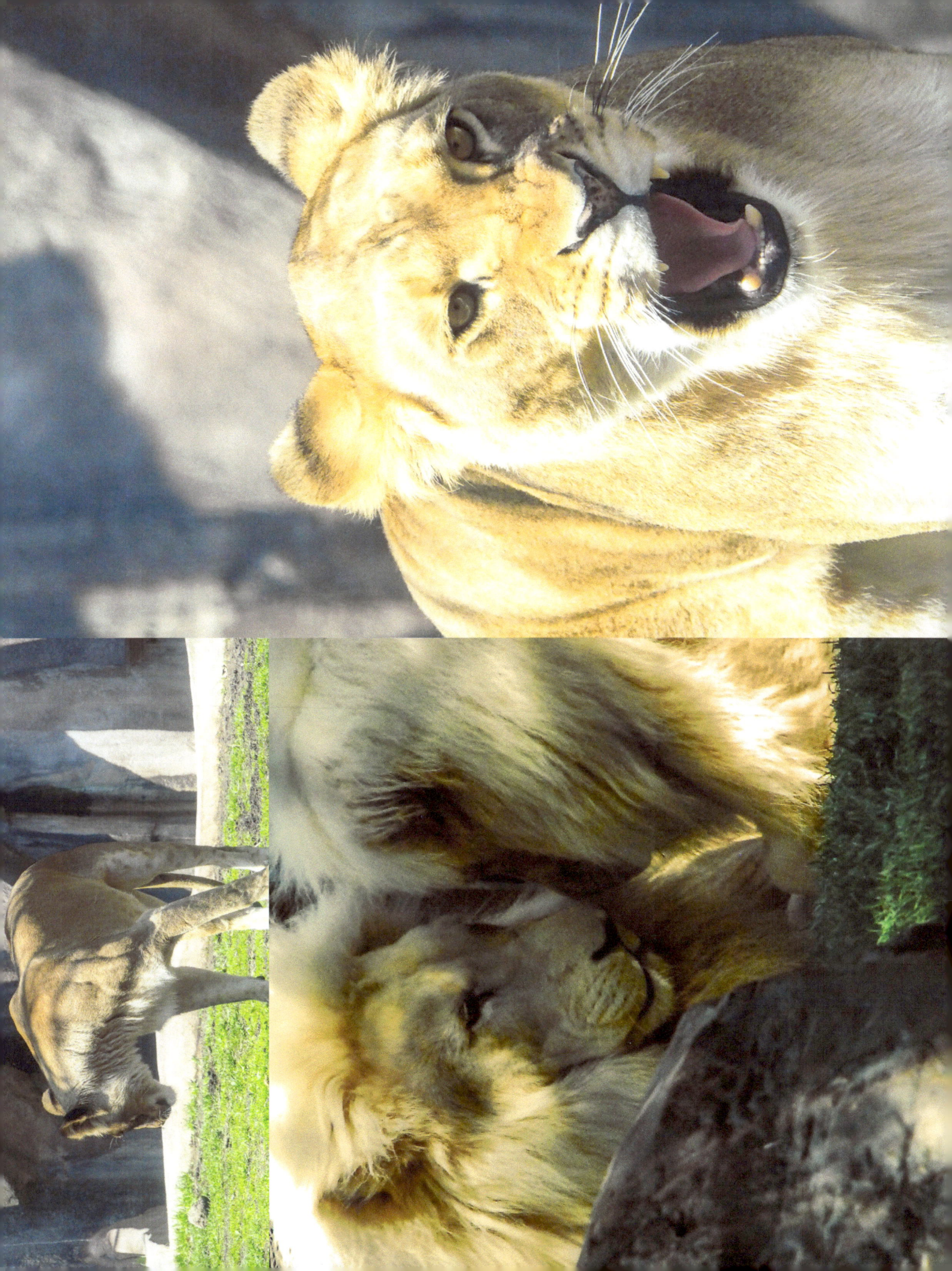

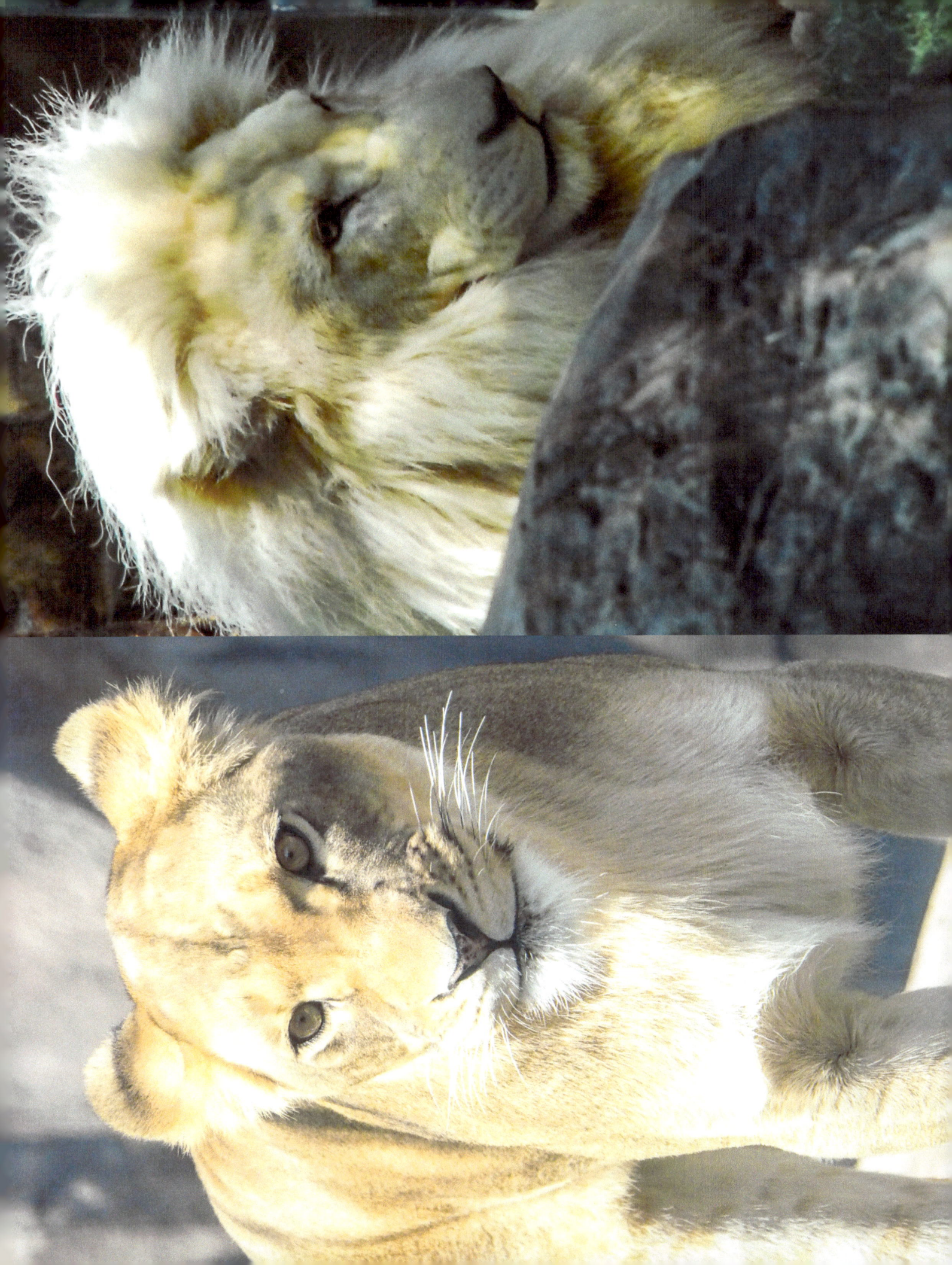

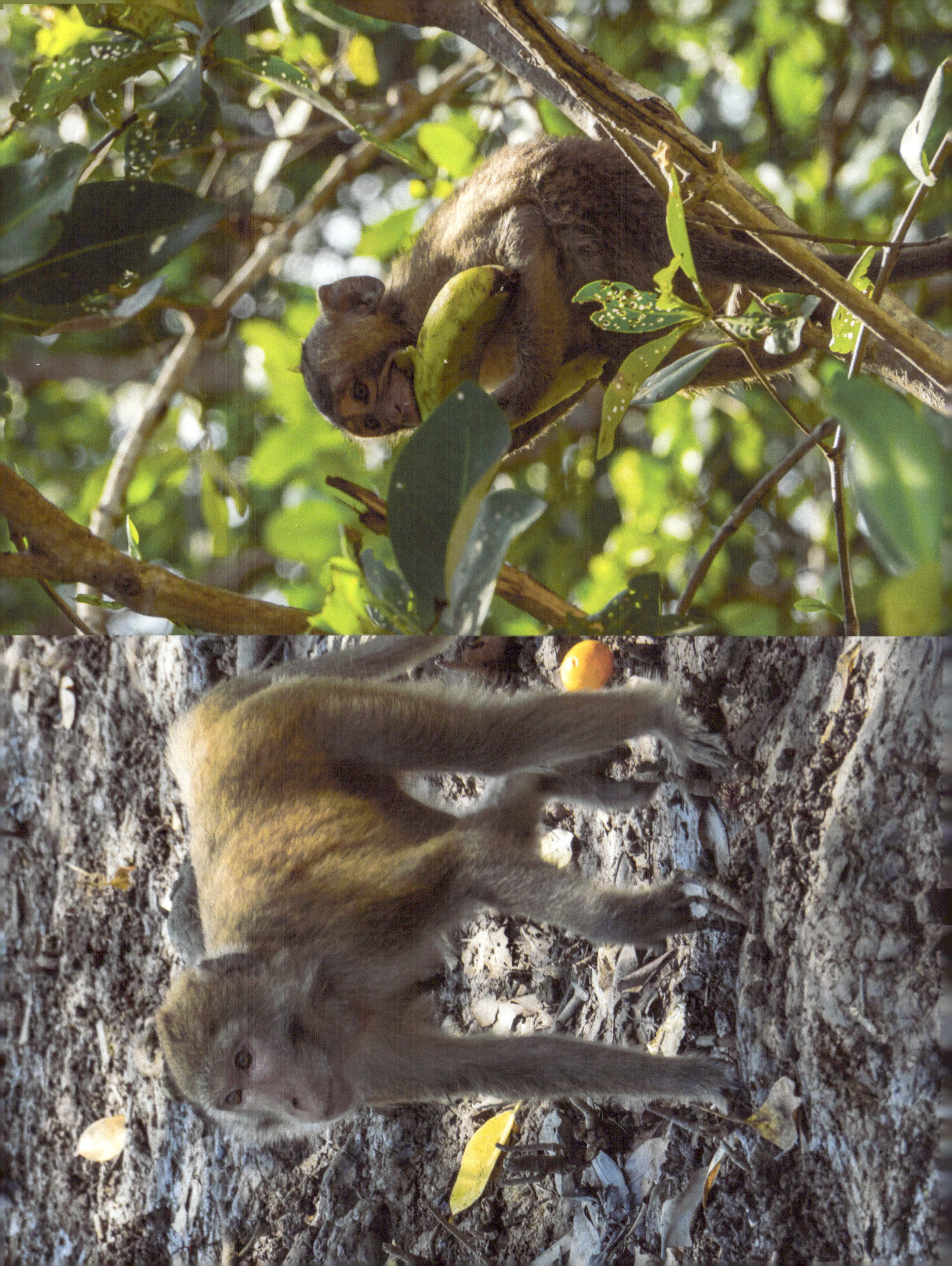

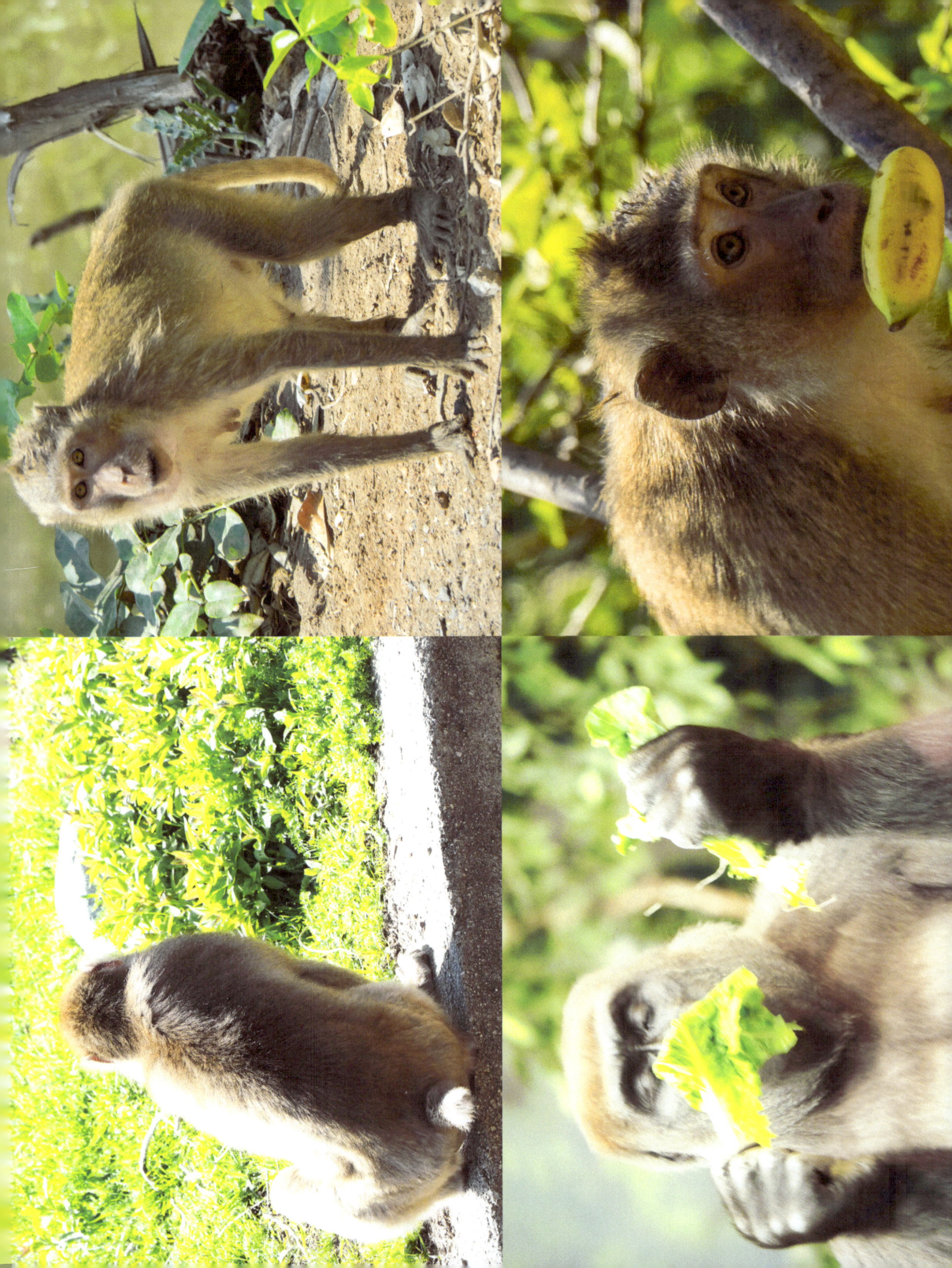

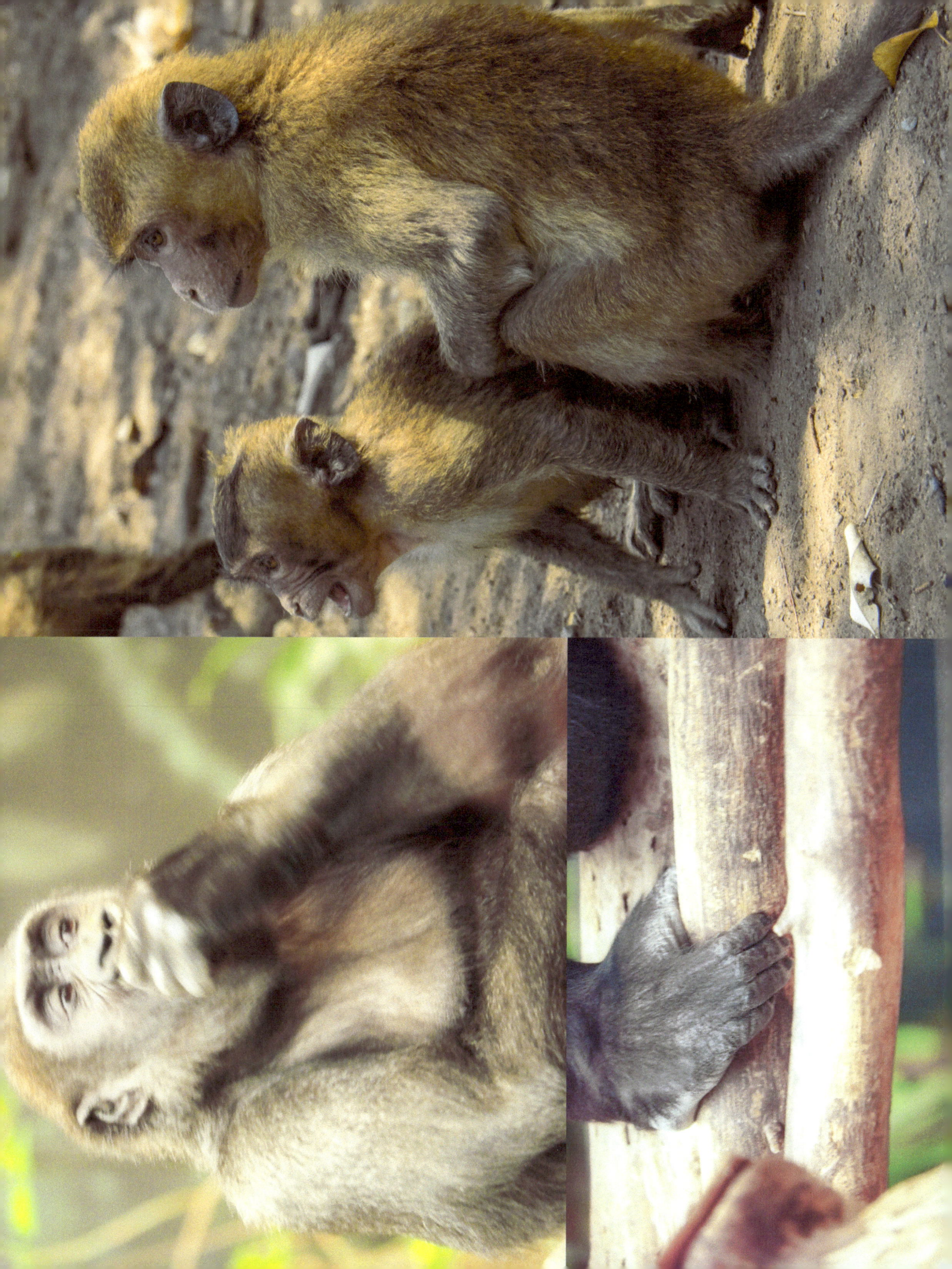

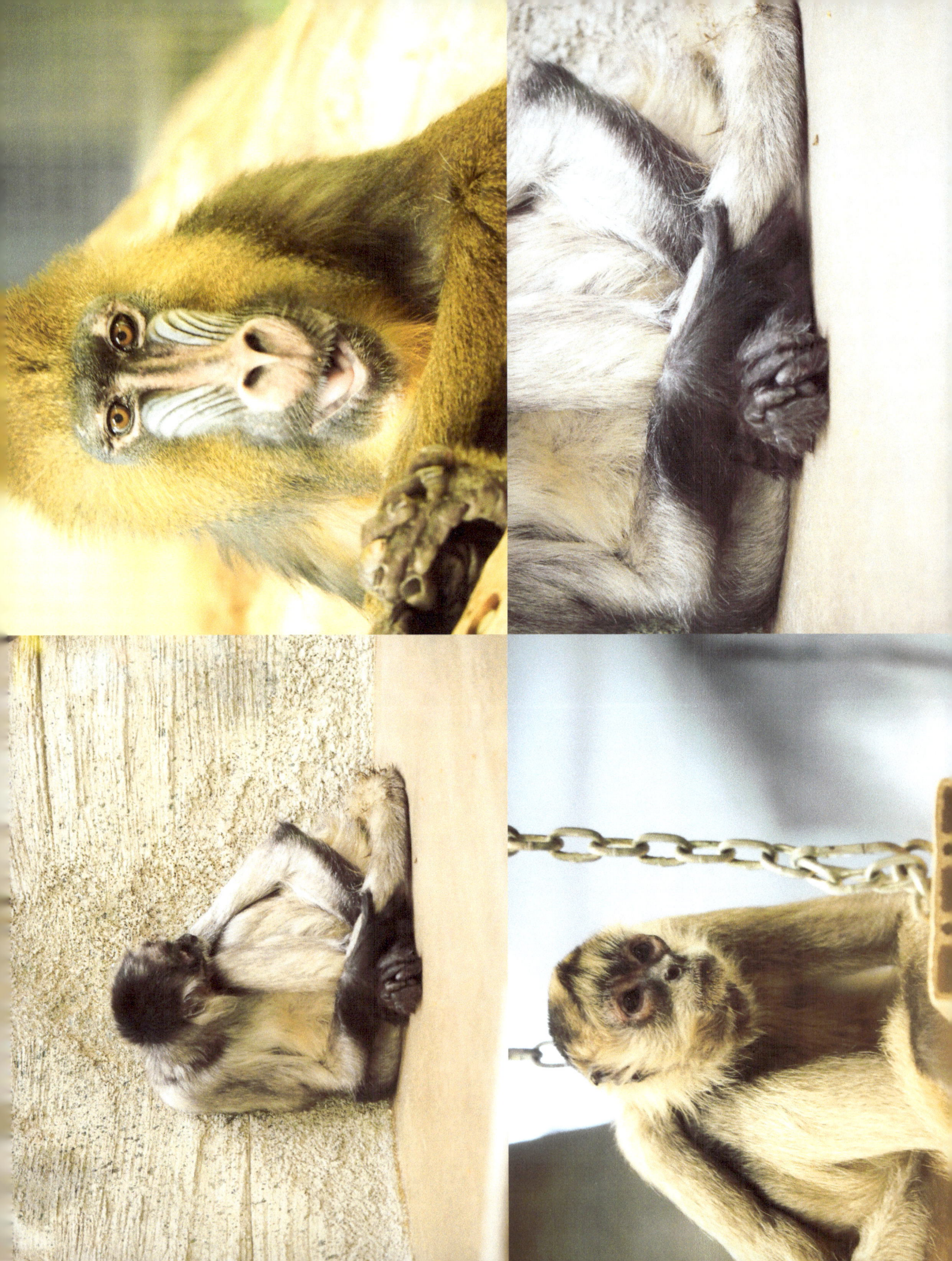

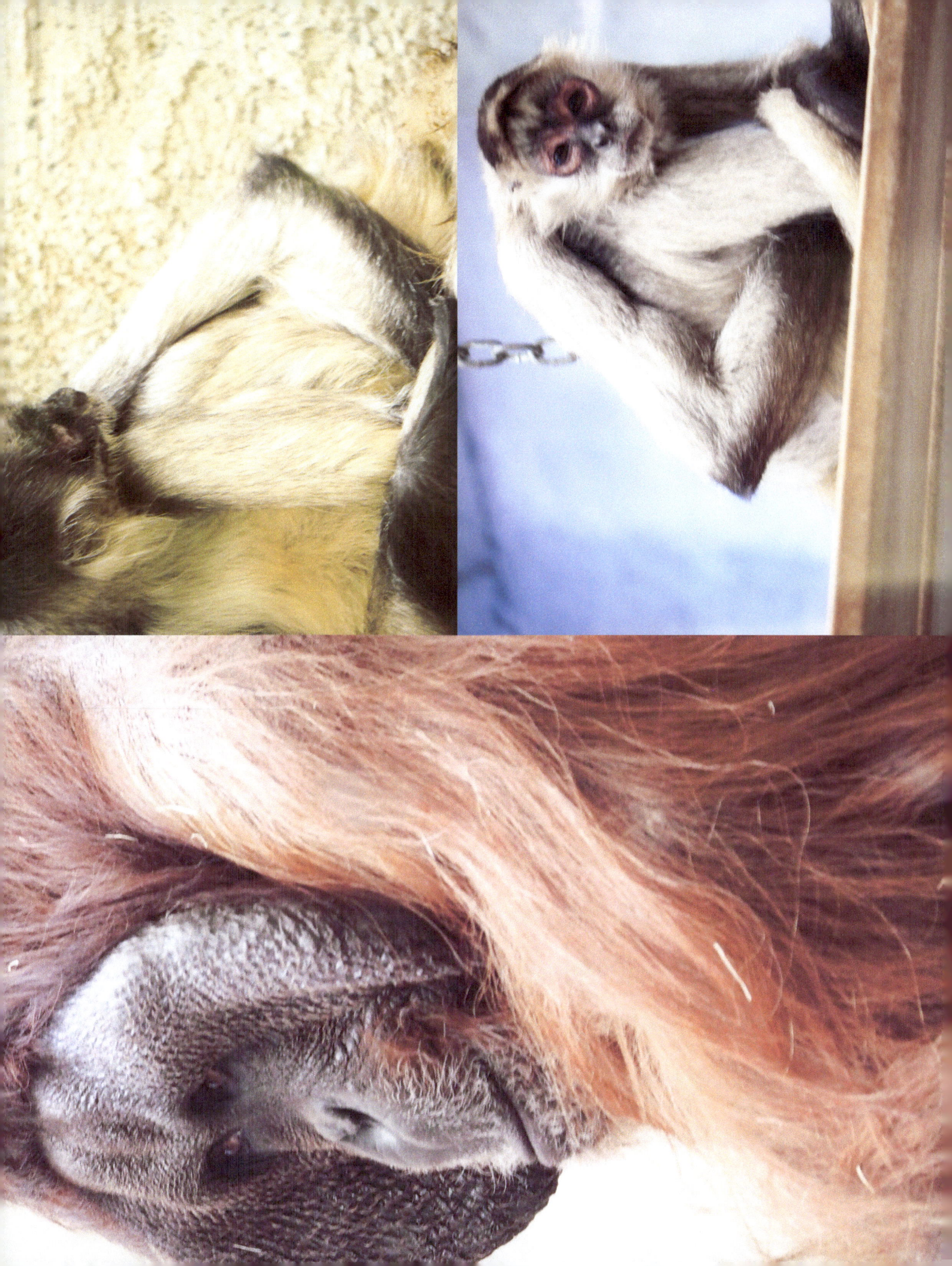

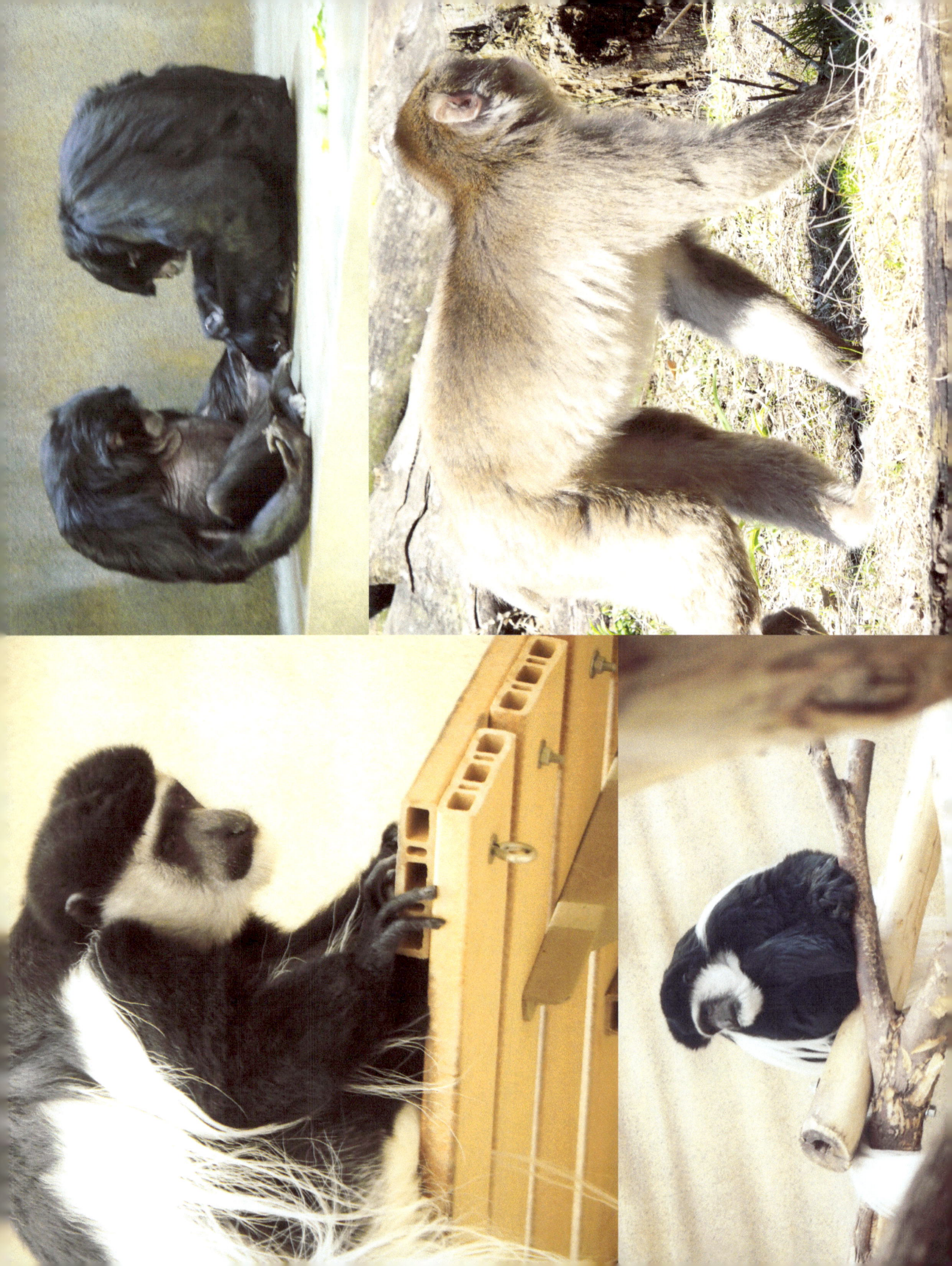

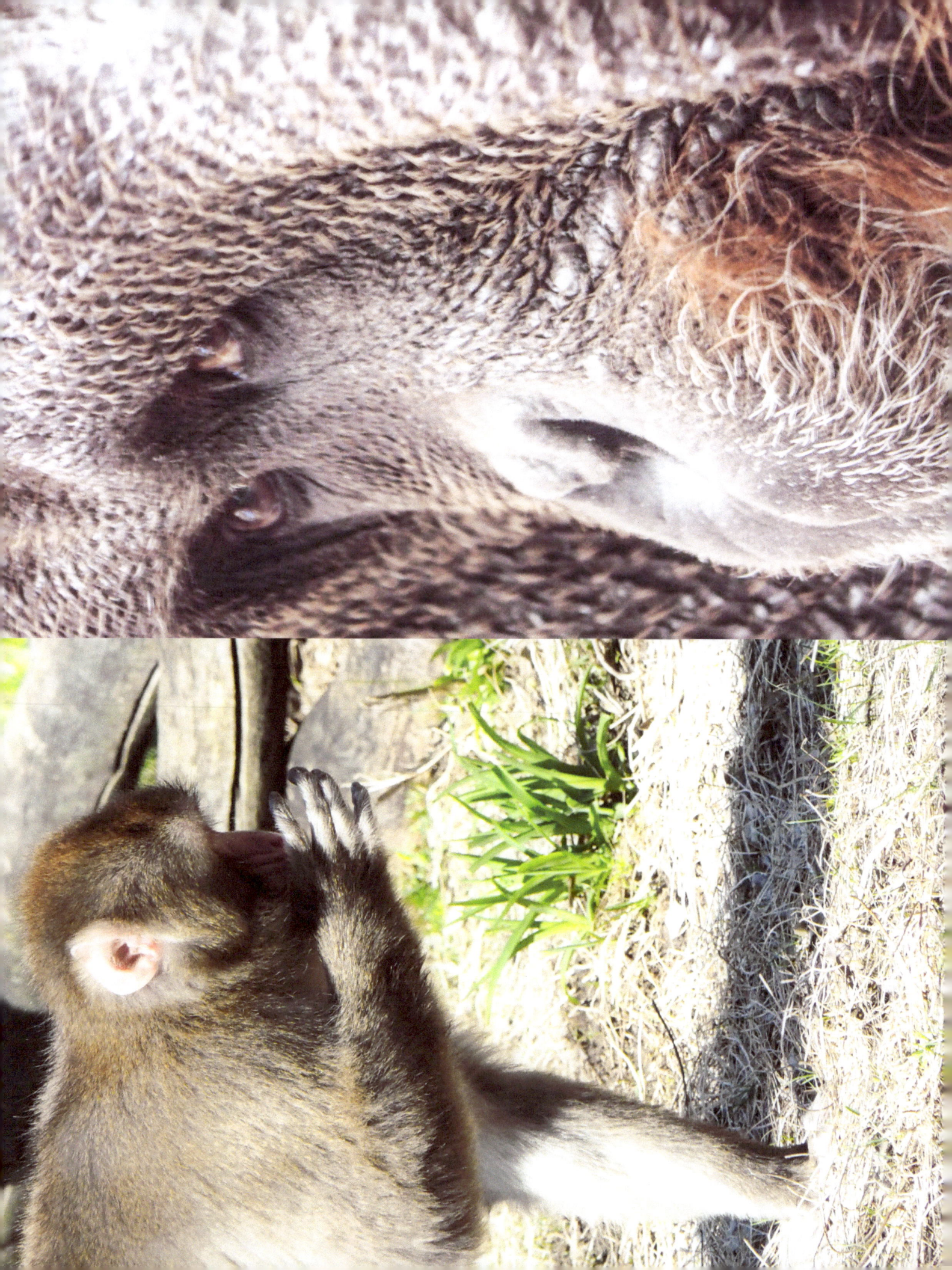

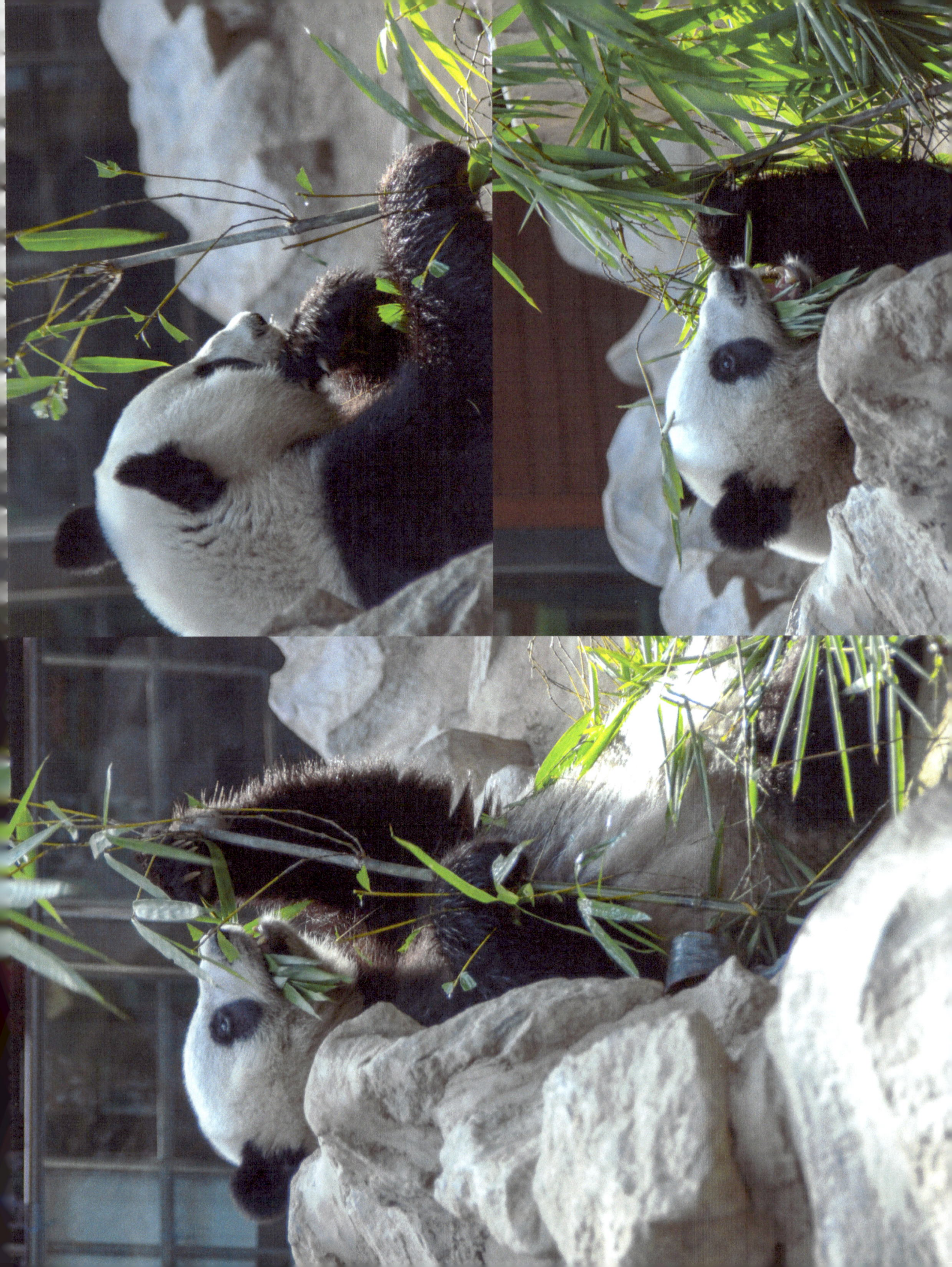

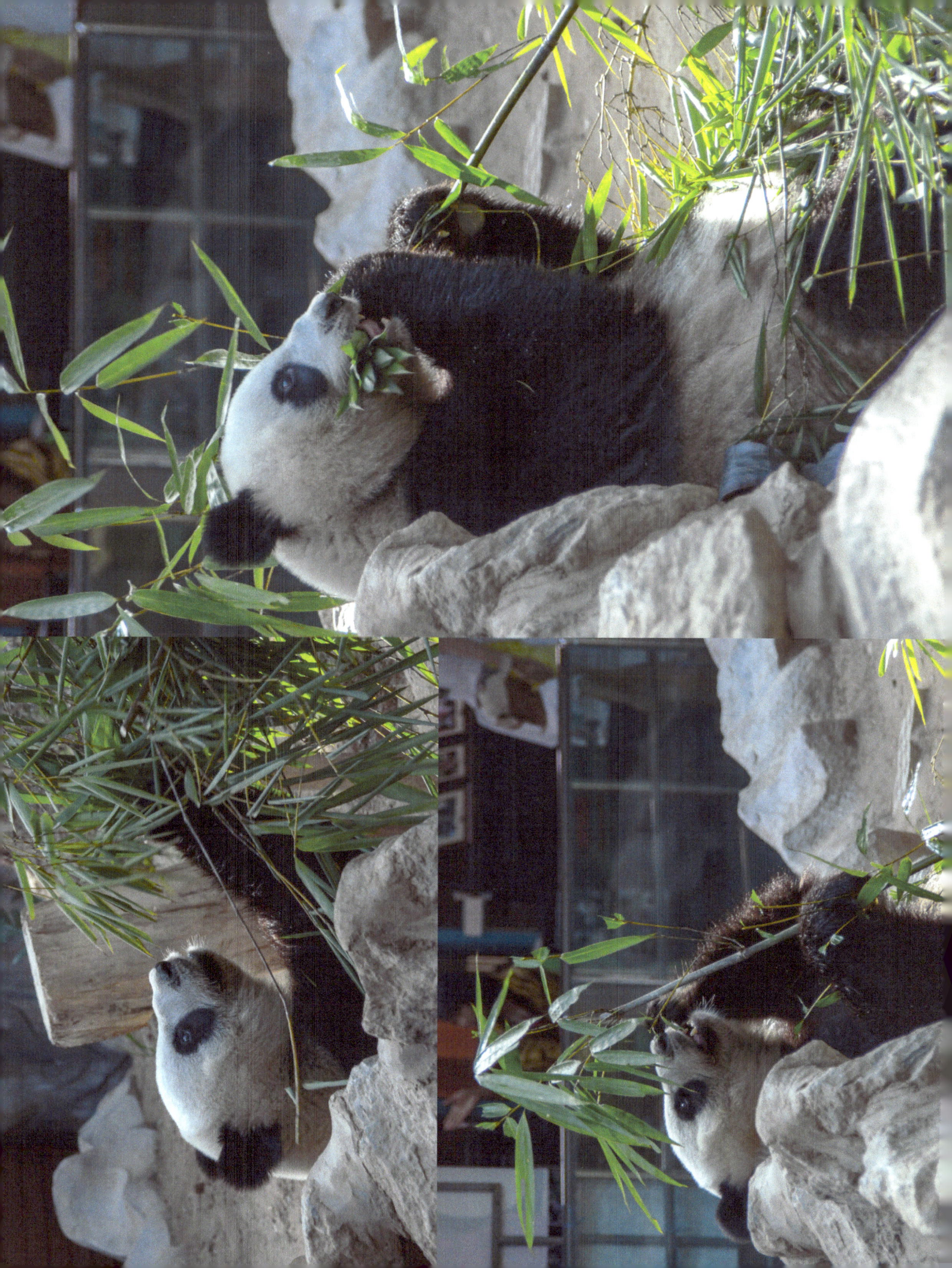

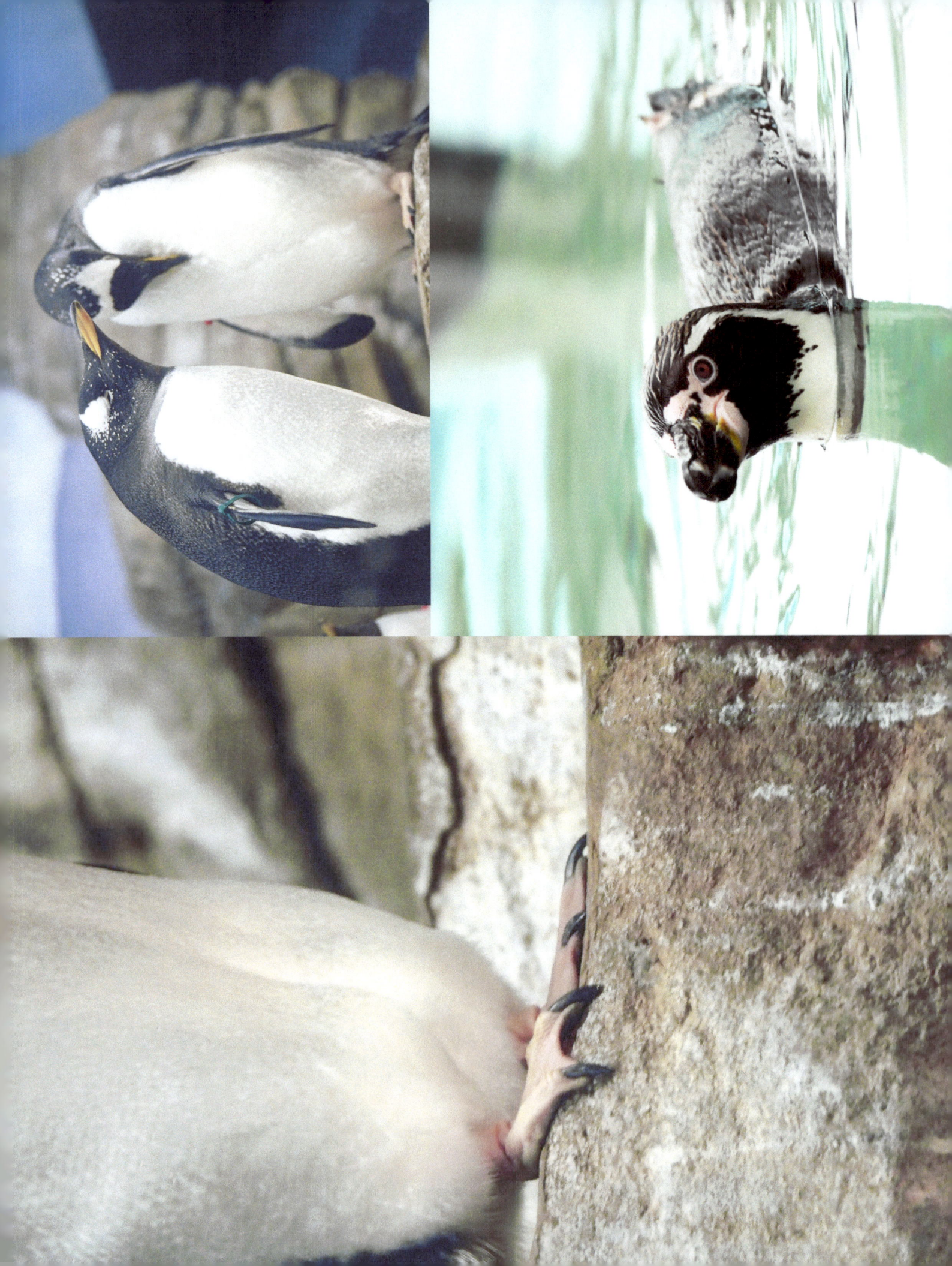

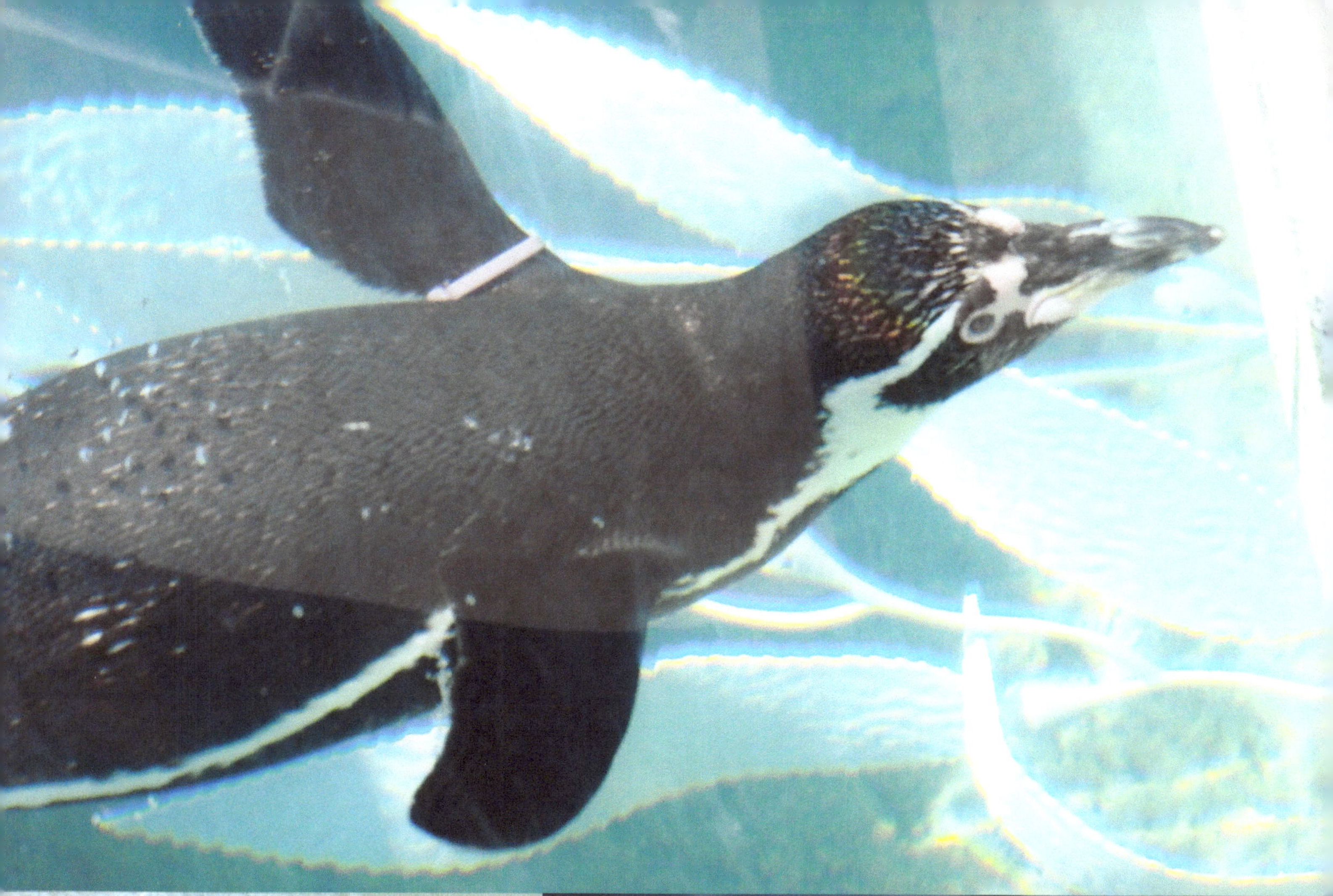

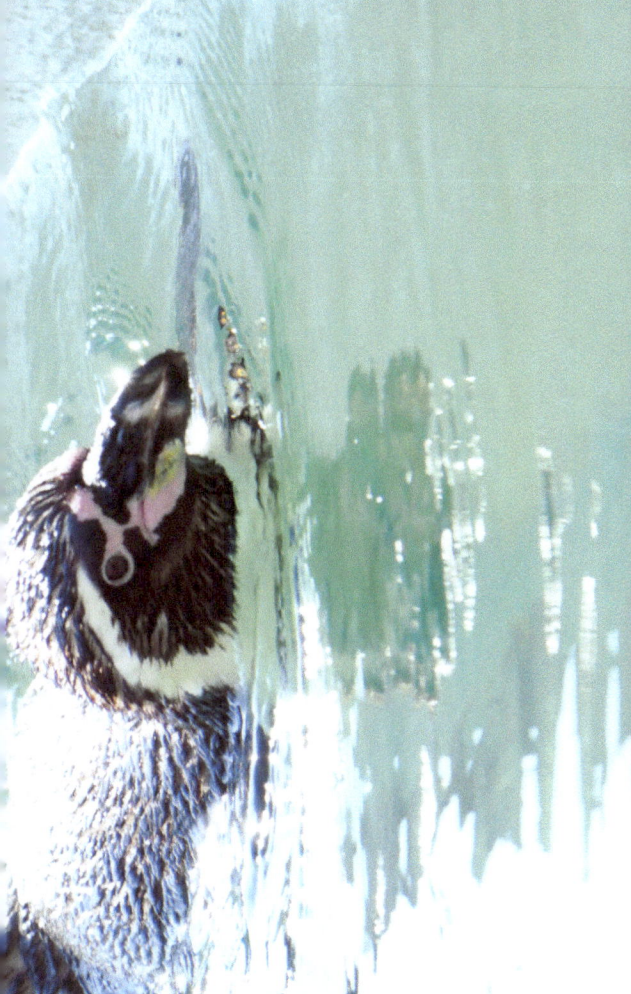
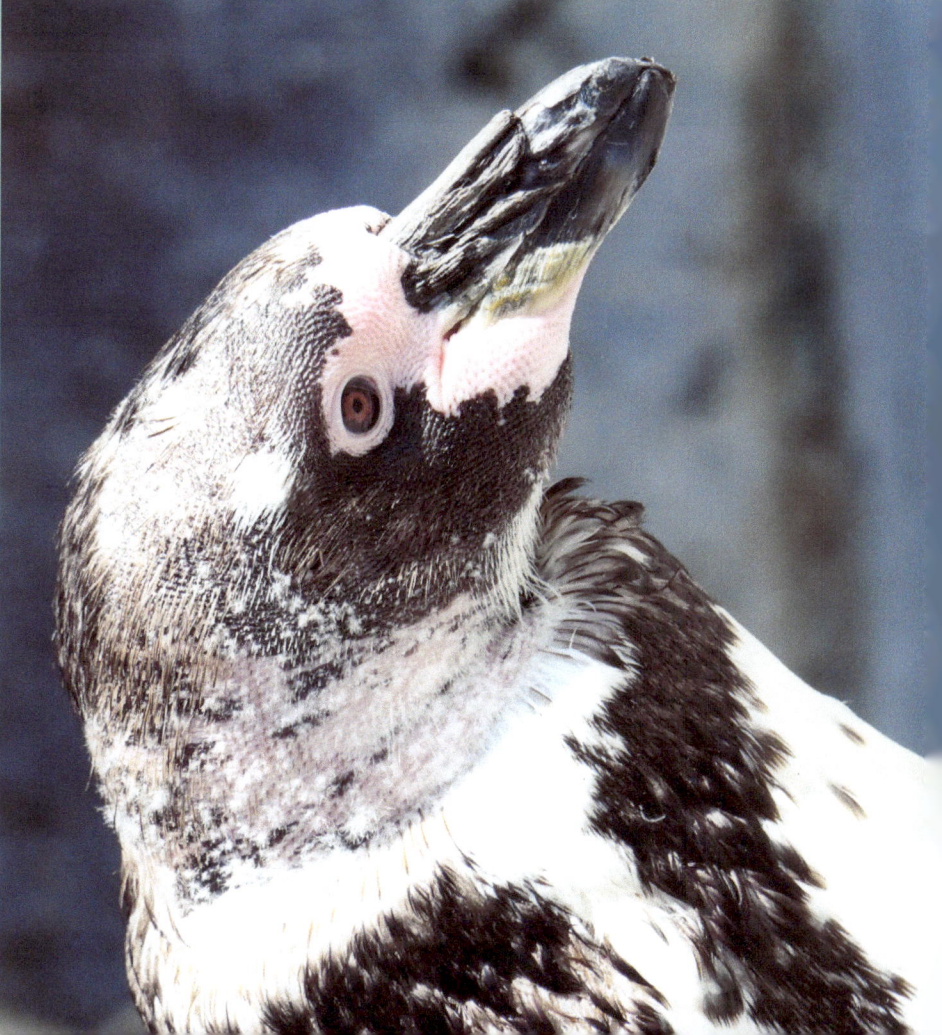

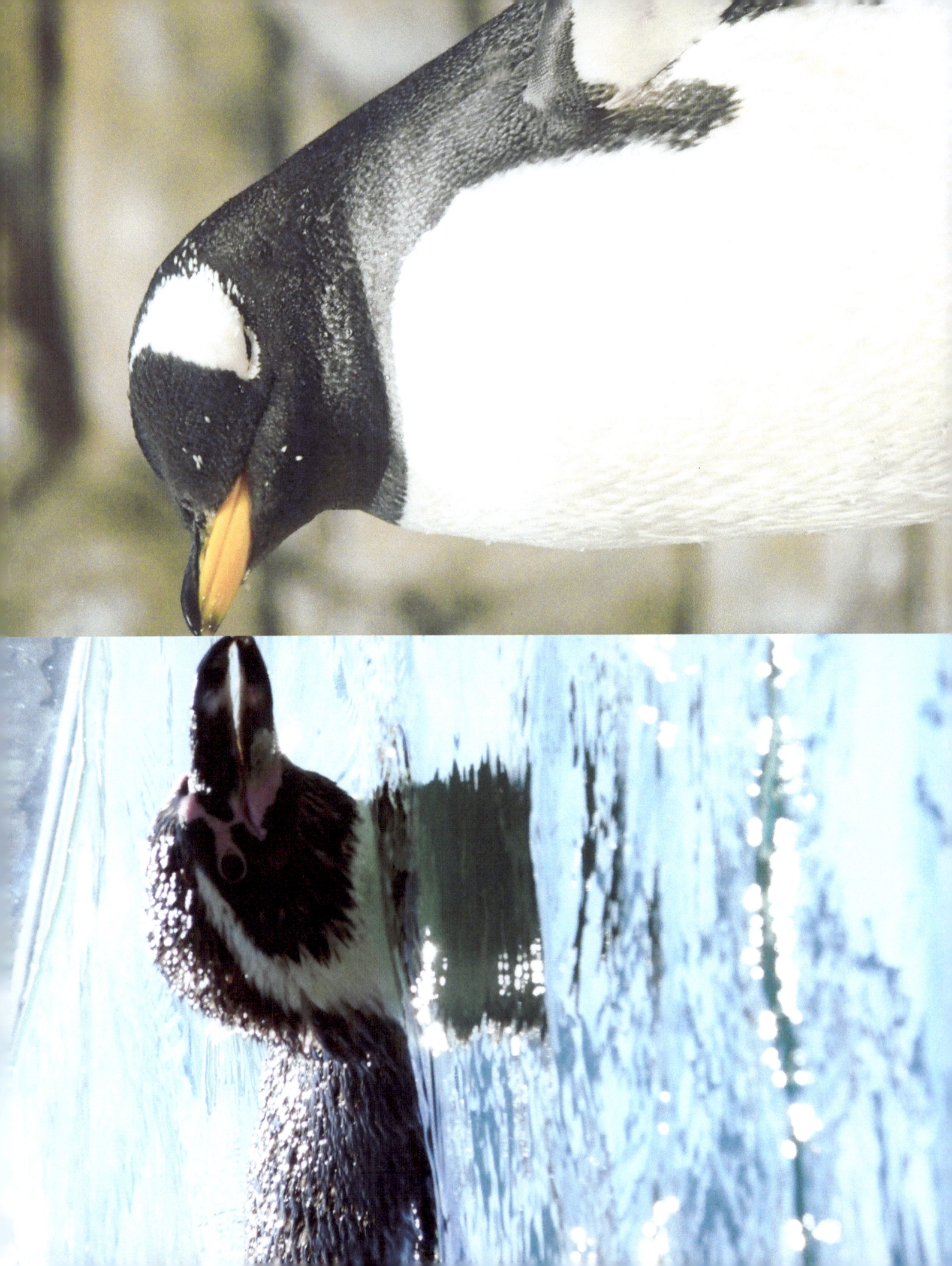

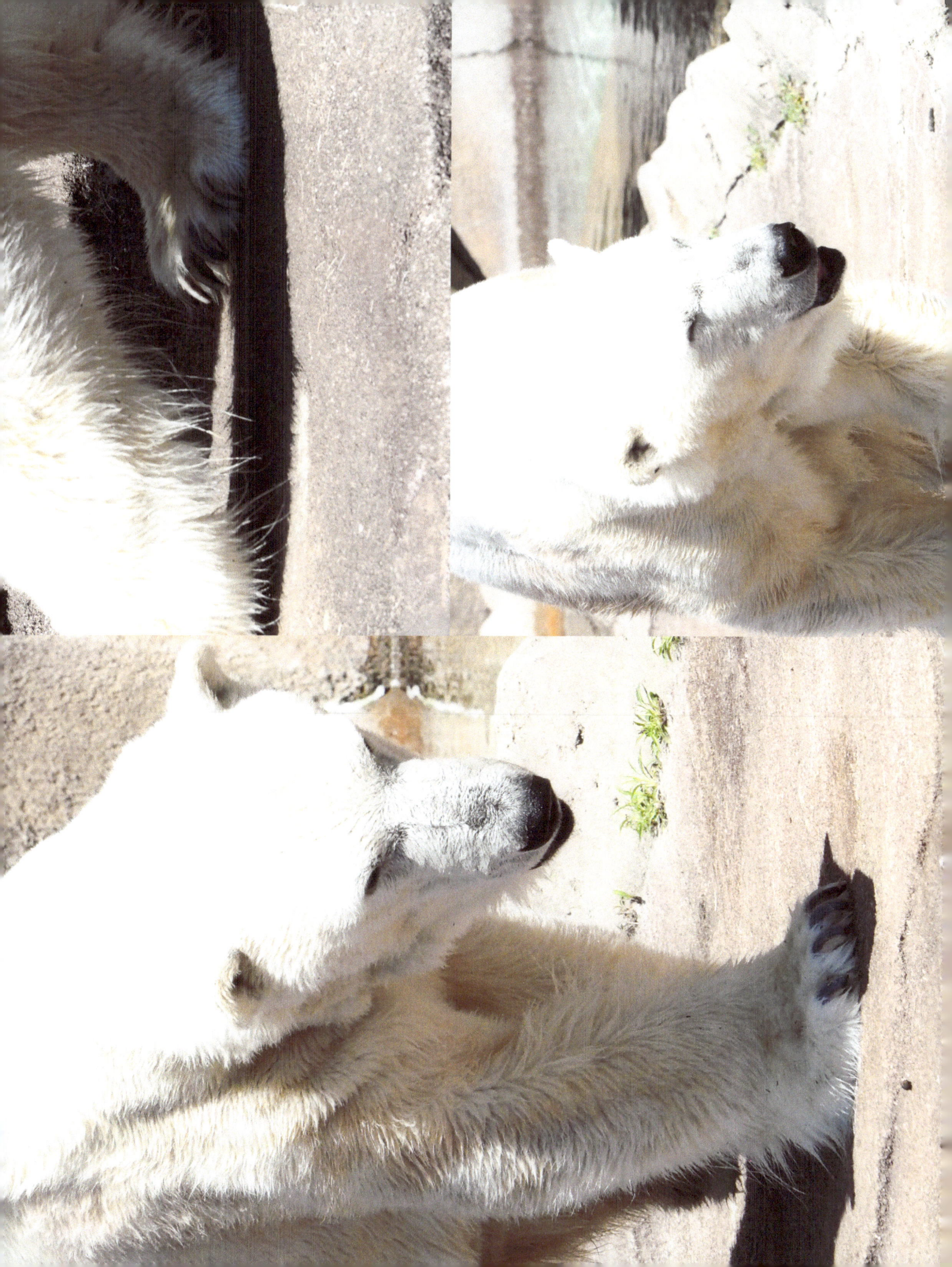

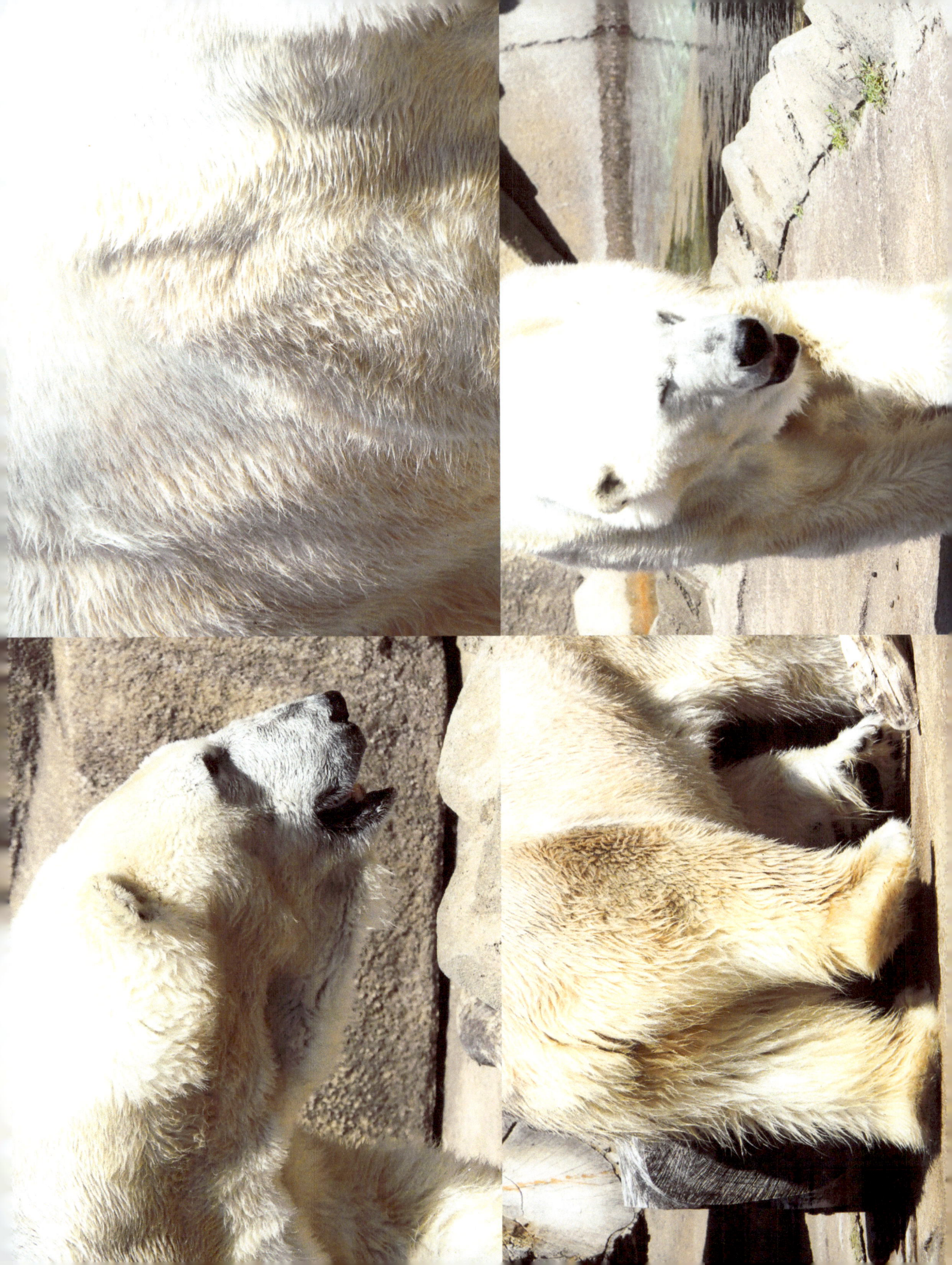

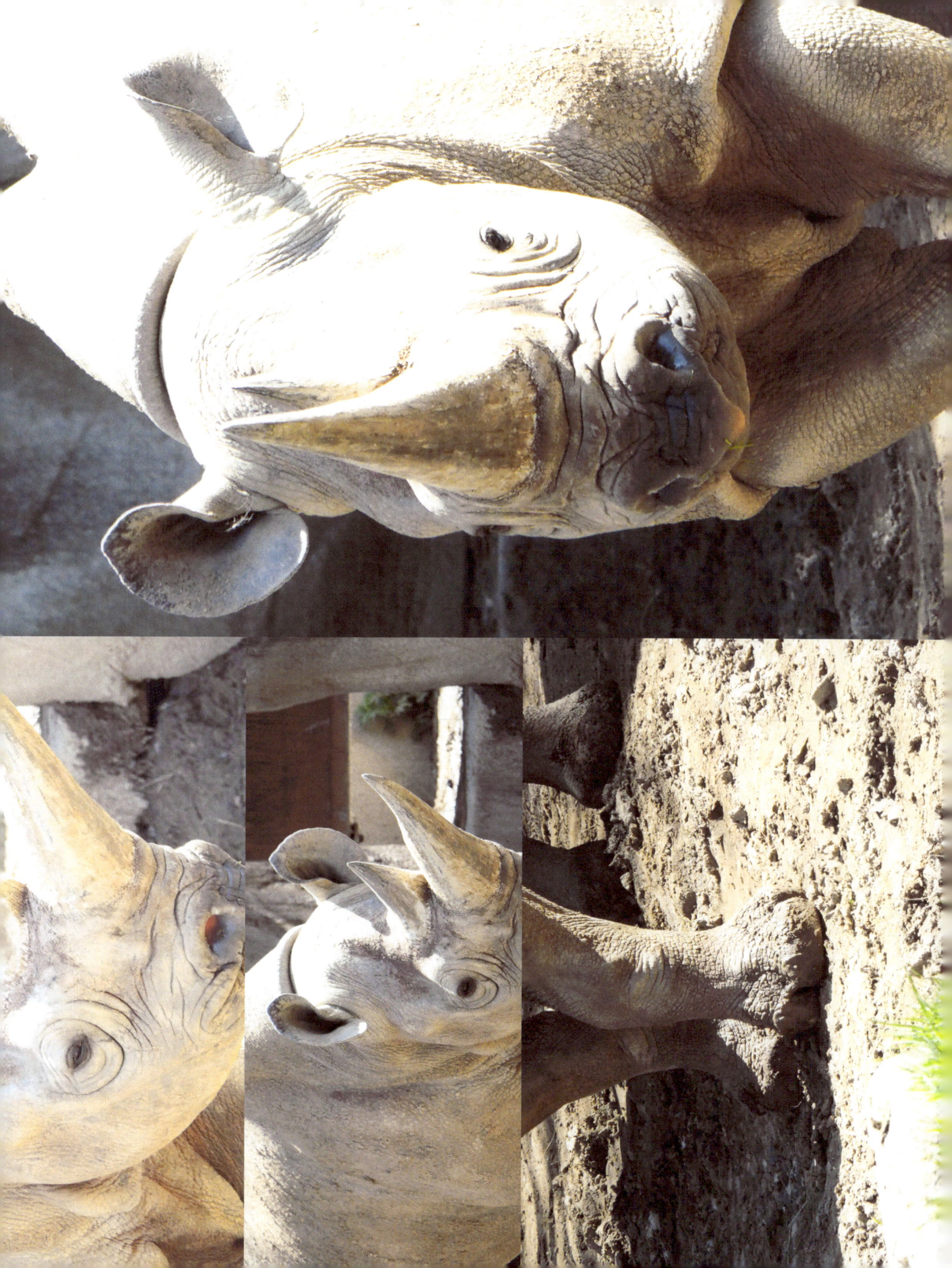

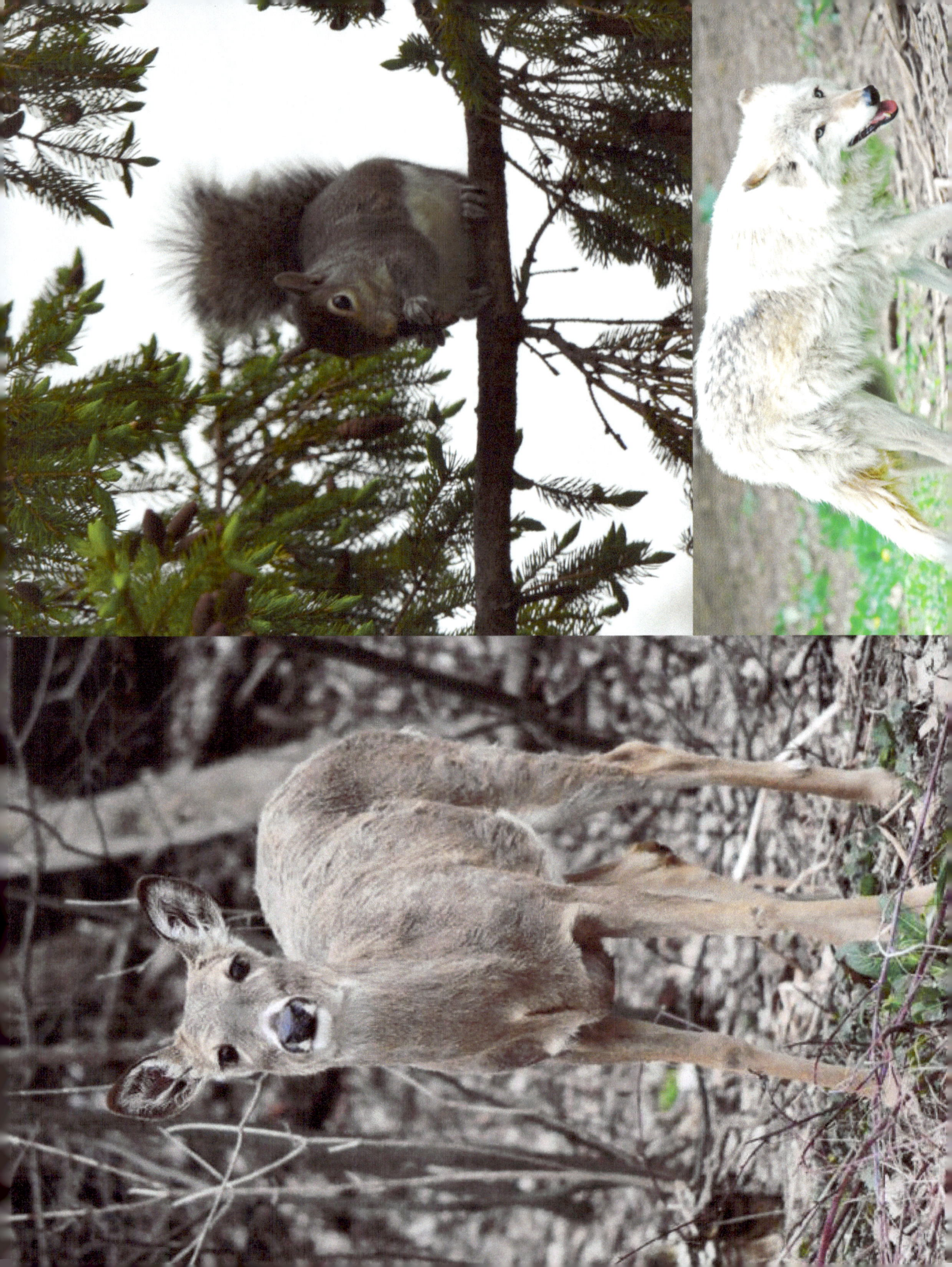

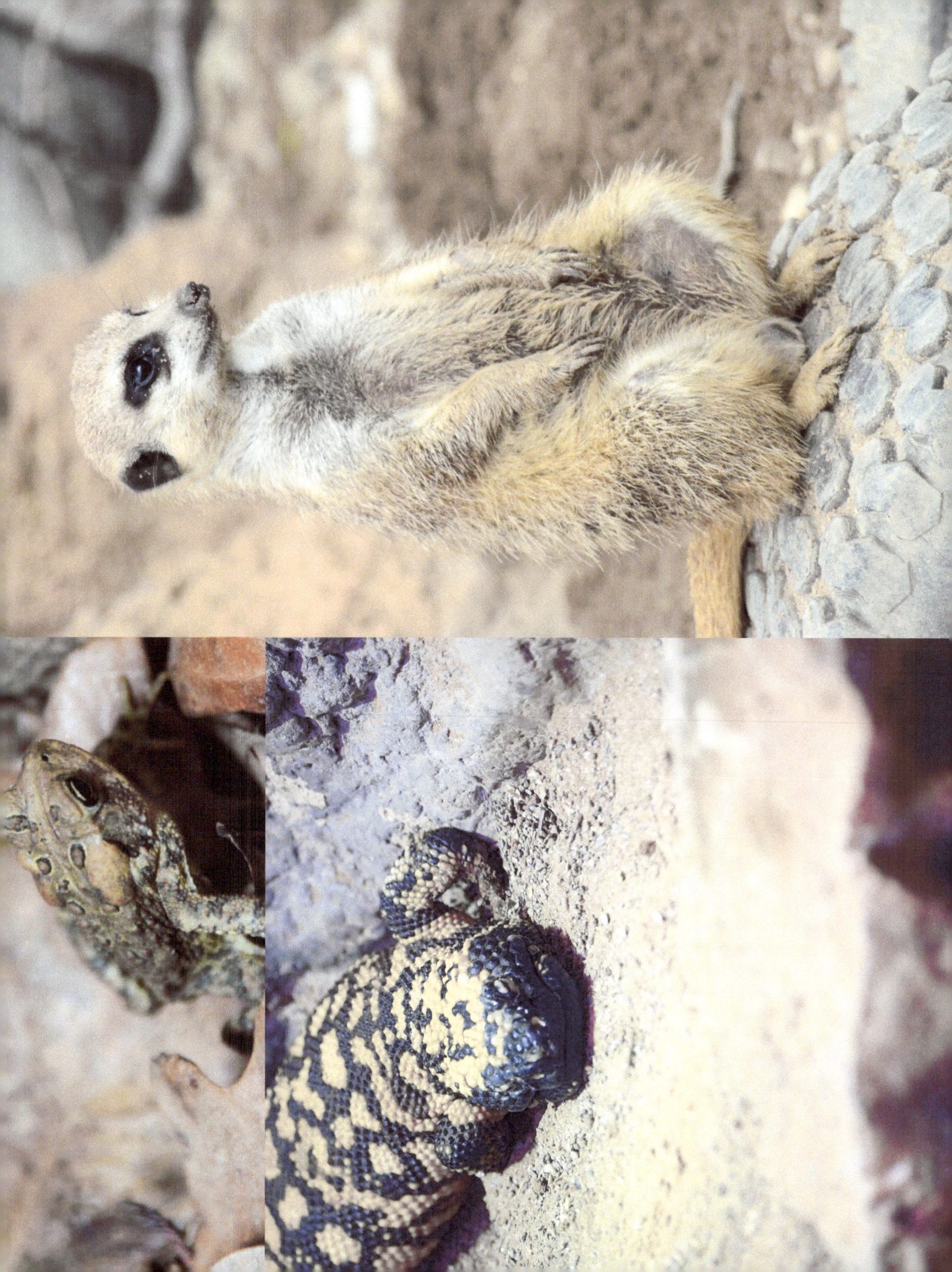

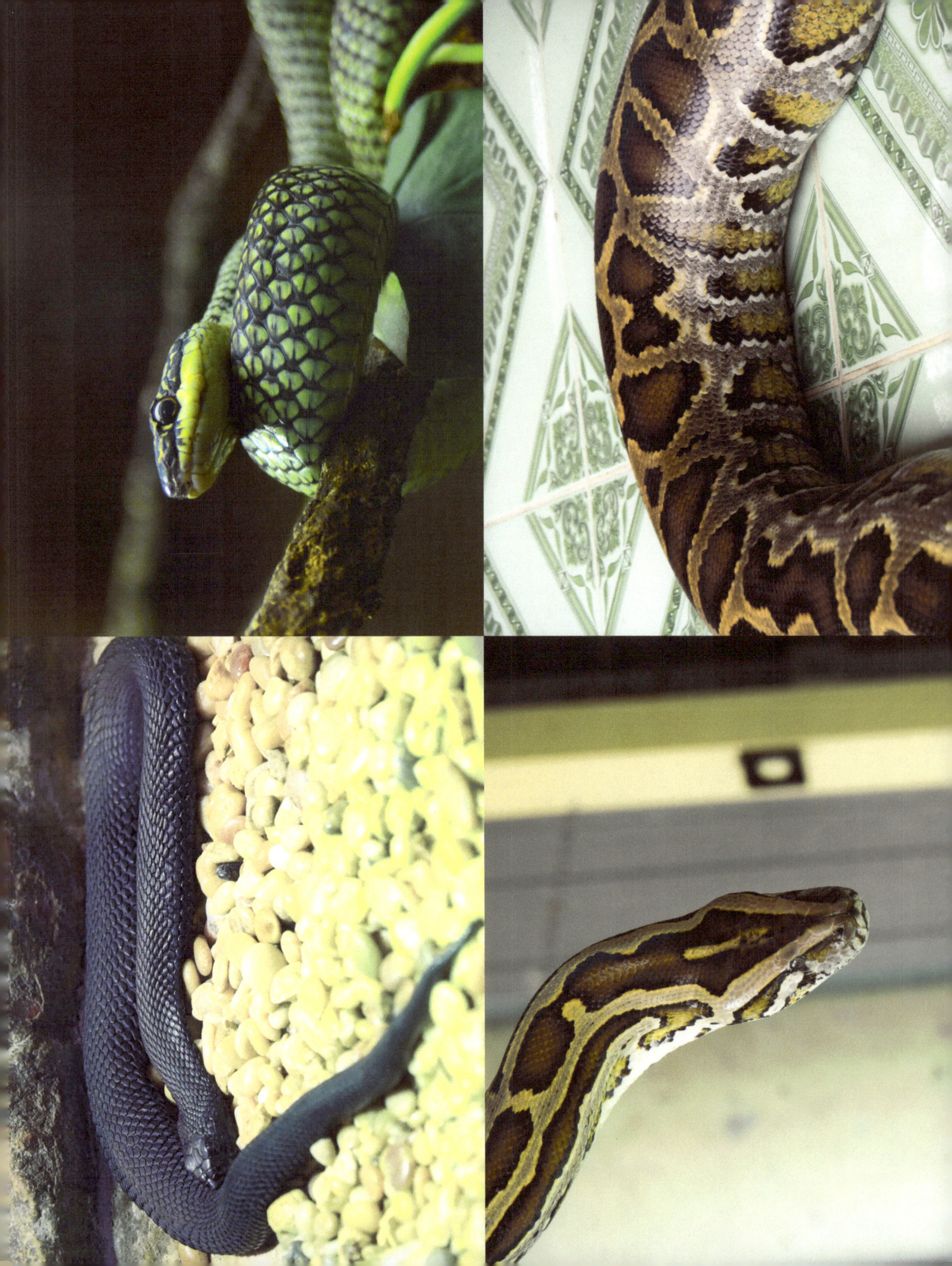

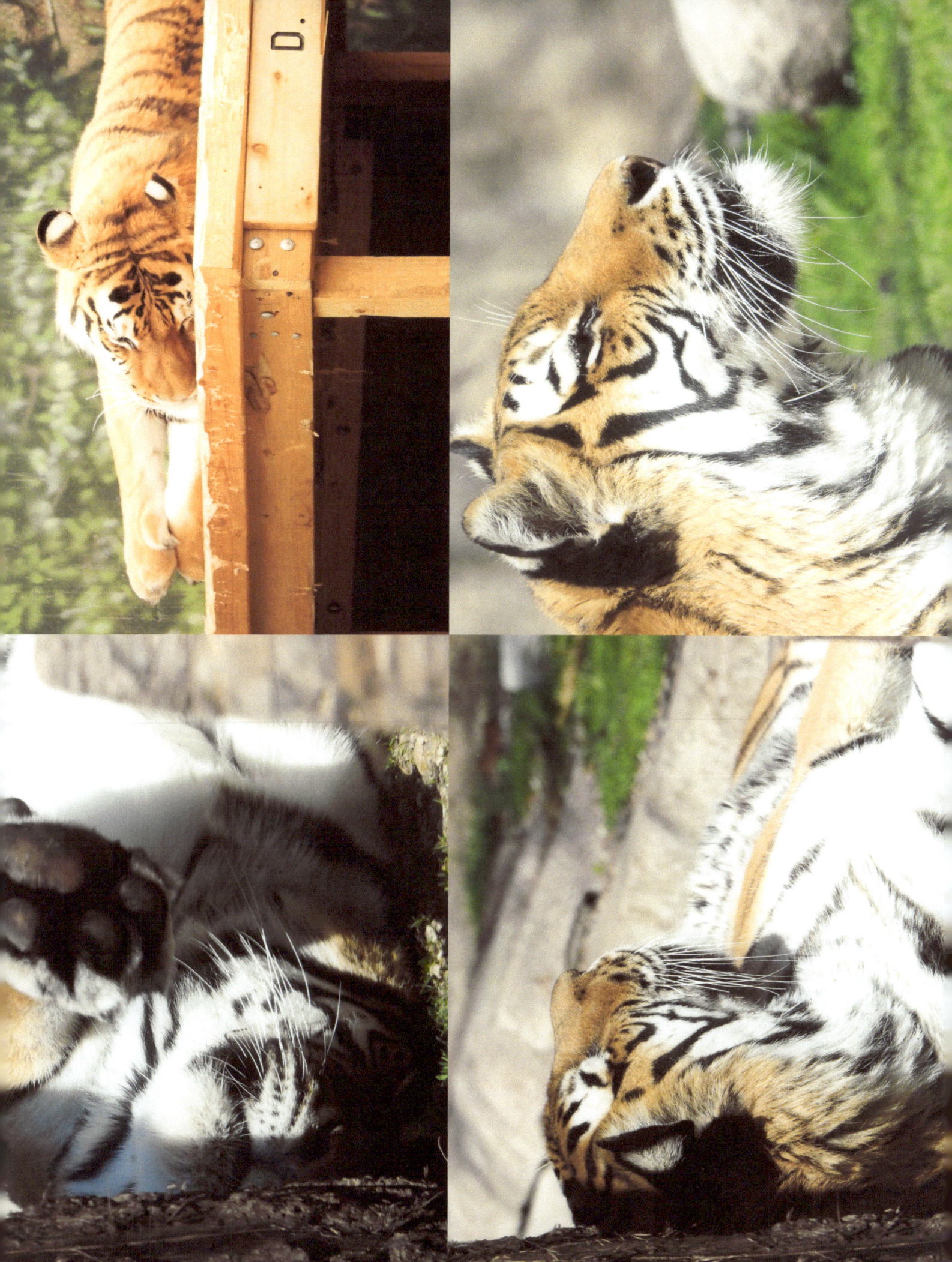

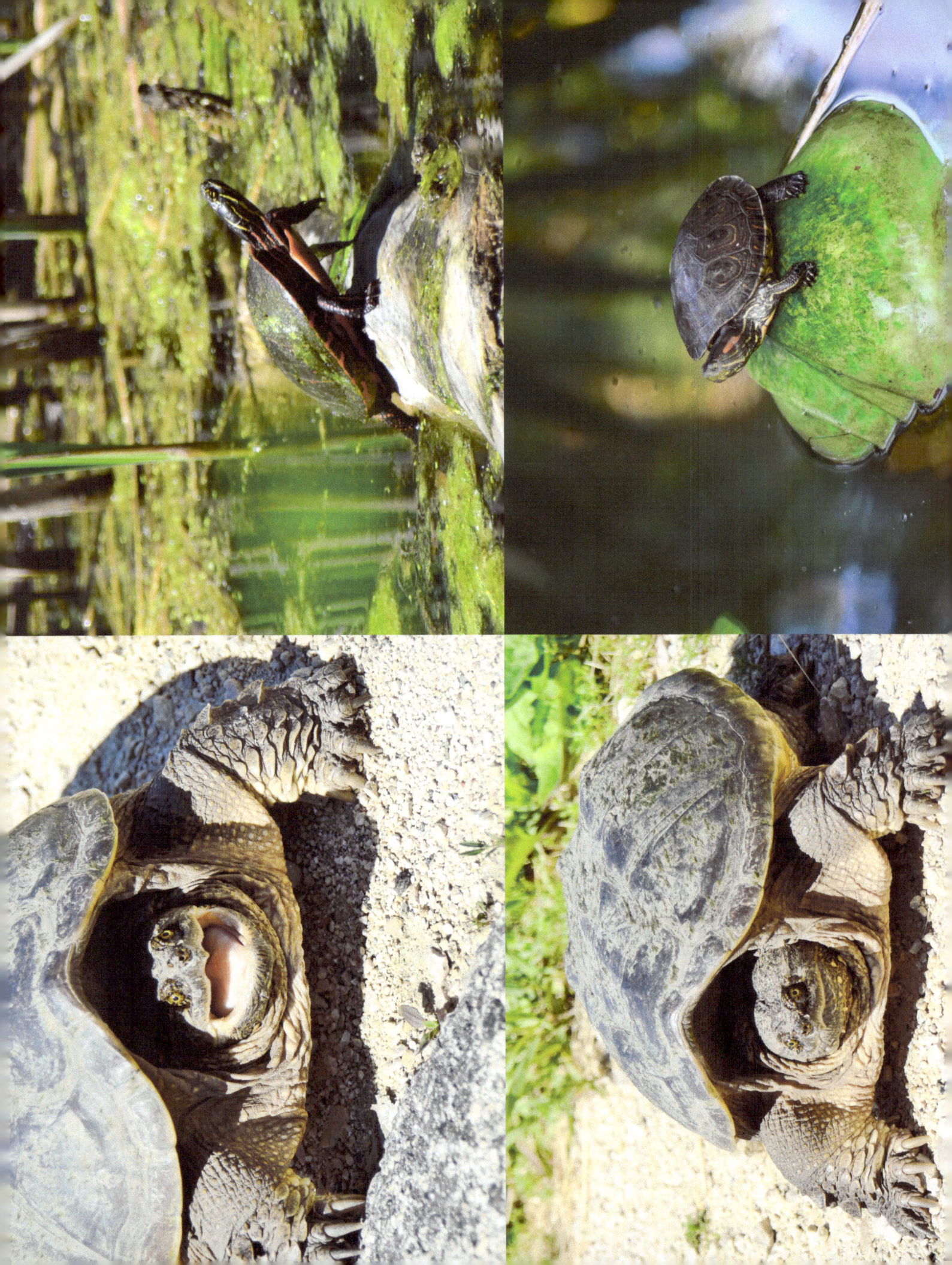

Photos for Creative Purposes
Available on Amazon

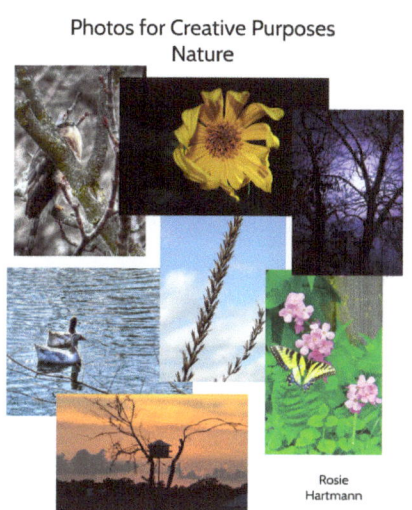
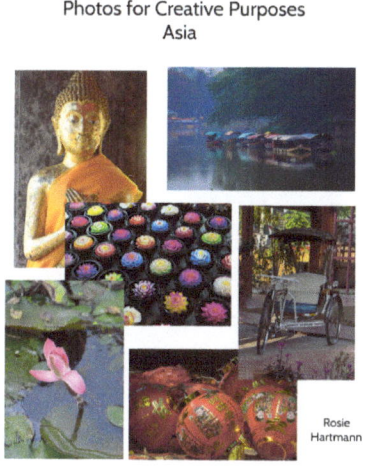
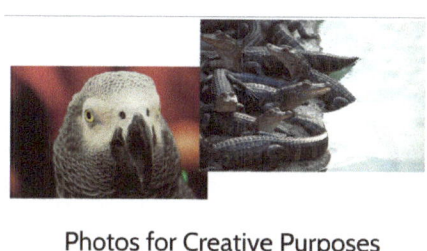
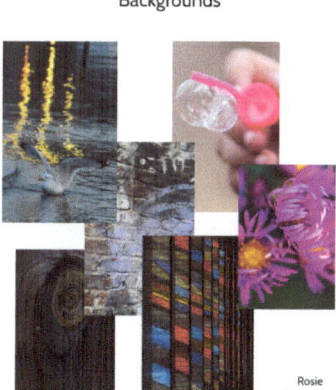
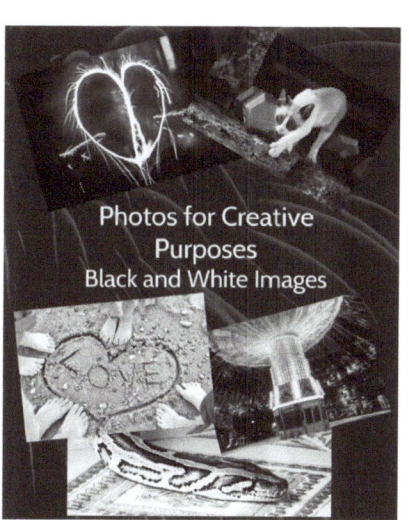

Follow us
Facebook: @StudioRosie

Have ideas for other topics?
email suggestions to christ@studiorosie.com